GEEKS BEARING GIFTS

GEEKS BEARING GIFTS

IMAGINING NEW FUTURES FOR NEWS

JEFF JARVIS

The City University of New York
CUNYJOURNALISM
PRESS

CUNY GRADUATE SCHOOL
TOW-KNIGHT OF JOURNALISM
CENTER FOR
ENTREPRENEURIAL
JOURNALISM

CUNY JOURNALISM PRESS IS THE ACADEMIC IMPRINT OF THE CUNY GRADUATE
SCHOOL OF JOURNALISM, PART OF THE CITY UNIVERSITY OF NEW YORK
219 WEST 40TH STREET, NEW YORK, NY 10018
WWW.PRESS.JOURNALISM.CUNY.EDU

First printing 2014

Cataloging-in-Publication data is available from the Library of Congress.
A catalog record for this book is available from the British Library.

ISBN 978-1-939293-73-2 paperback
ISBN 978-1-939293-74-9 e-book

Cover and text design by Bathcat Ltd. Typeset by CBIGS Group, Chennai,
India. Printed by BookMobile in the United States and CPI Books Ltd in
the United Kingdom.

For Steve Shepard —
dean, editor, mentor, sounding board, supporter, friend.
(It's all his fault.)

CONTENTS

INTRODUCTION

NEW RELATIONSHIPS, FORMS, AND MODELS FOR NEWS

These digital visionaries tell people like me that we just don't understand them. They talk about the wonders of the interconnected world, about the democratization of journalism. The news, they say, is viral now — that we should be grateful. Well, I think all of us need to beware of geeks bearing gifts. Here we are in 2009 — more viral, less profitable. Because news costs. Because quality costs. Because free sets the price too low. Because free isn't sustainable. Because free is too expensive.

—LES HINTON, THEN CEO OF DOW JONES, SPEAKING TO THE
WORLD NEWSPAPER CONGRESS IN HYDERABAD, INDIA, DEC. 1, 2009[1]

I am grateful for geeks' gifts to news. Technology provides no end of opportunities for improving, expanding, reimagining, and sustaining news. Yes, technology has also disrupted the news industry — its relationships, forms, and business models. But in this essay, I will try not to dwell on the fleeting past. In their white paper, *The Story So Far: What We Know About the Business of Digital Journalism*, Bill Grueskin and his coauthors at Columbia's School of Journalism examined how our industry arrived at where we are today.[2] Also from Columbia's Tow Center, *Post-Industrial Journalism: Adapting to the Present* by Emily Bell, Clay Shirky, and Chris Anderson proposed ways for news organizations to exploit the opportunities that technology presents today to update, expand, and improve the craft.[3] I now want to look to the future. Or rather, I want to examine many possible futures. I don't want to predict where journalism will go. But I do want to imagine where it can go next and what is possible in the future.

After the invention of that great disruptive technology, the printing press, it took half a century for the book to take its own form. At the start, printers still mimicked scribes' work, using fonts designed to duplicate their handwriting. Printing was initially promoted as "automated writing." We still define the future in the terms of the past. Cars were "horseless carriages" propelled by "horsepower." Radio was named what it wasn't: "the wireless." Today, we still "dial" and "hang up" phones, though those words have long since lost their literal meanings. For that matter, how soon will it be before it seems absurd to call smartphones "phones" when less and less we use them to talk and more and more we use them as — what? — computers, connectors, assistants, brains. . . .

On the internet today, newspapers, magazines, books, radio, and TV are each still substantially recognizable as their own forebears. Many have moved past the first phase of adaptation — shovelware, or simply pouring old wine into new skins — to take advantage of online's added functionality. There was much oohing[4] and aahing[5] over a New York Times story about an avalanche with slideshows, video, photographic aerial maps, and graphics embedded in the tale.[6] It's lovely. But it still does what journalists do: It tells a story. It was still possible for The Times to print the narrative in the newspaper with little lost. We have arrived at what some may consider a destination but I hope is merely a way station: the fulfillment of multimedia storytelling. I'd like for us to look past the story; now the article is but one tool available to us to do the work of journalism. We must continue the search for what is possible today that was not possible before, to find new ways to serve the public, and to find new models to sustain that work. In this essay, I will try to rethink media and its opportunities, putting my own stake in the ground to imagine various futures and to respond to the challenge I hear often: "So, smartass, now that your damned beloved internet has ruined news, what next?"

The Columbia Journalism Review has accused me, along with New York University's Jay Rosen and Clay Shirky and Columbia's Emily Bell, of conspiring in a Future of News (FON) cabal.[7] "At its heart, the FON consensus is anti-institutional. It believes that old institutions must wither to make way for the networked future," CJR said. "The establishment has no plan. The FON consensus says no plan *is* the plan. The establishment drones on about rules and standards; the FON thinkers talk about freedom and informality." When I met the author of that characterization, Dean Starkman, at a Baruch College event in 2012, I readily confessed that I have no damned idea what the future of news will be.[8] No one does.

If I had a plan, I'd be eliminating possibilities. I'd be predicting the future and prescribing it. But I'm not trying to do that. If we define the future today, we'll do so in the terms of our past. Horseless carriages. We still have more imagining to do. That's what this essay is: an exercise in personal brainstorming — one I'd like to see undertaken by journalism students, journalism teachers, journalists, publishers, media companies, technologists, investors, activists, and anyone who cares about news and society. If we don't imagine many futures, we can't build any. We must start by questioning three key industrial assumptions about news, or we'll never get past trying to preserve them.

- First, that the natural role of the public in relation to journalism is as the mass, as an audience — or as my friend Rosen calls them now, the people formerly known as the audience.[9] Who are they today? What roles can they play? How does this shift in roles affect the value of the journalist in this new relationship? In the first part of this essay, I will propose different perspectives for conceiving of the role of journalism in society: as a service, a builder of platforms, an organizer, an advocate, a teacher, an incubator. I will argue that journalism must learn how to get into the relationship business; that, I believe, can be a foundation for a new business strategy for the news industry.

- Second, that the article is the atomic unit and necessary product of news and that journalists are storytellers. Articles, I am sure, will remain a key tool journalists will use to add value to a flow of information — with narrative, organization, context, summary, example, and discussion. But in the second part of this essay, I will try to move past the article or story to examine other forms news may take: as data (our current darling) and also as functionality, as platforms, as sets of information assets with many paths through them, as curation, as conversations.

- The final assumption: That old business models can be recreated in a new reality, that newsrooms will (or won't) be preserved, that print won't (or will) survive, that people will or should (or won't) pay for news, that advertising must (or can't) support news, that media companies will control news (or die). I don't believe that news is in jeopardy. We see increased access to news, interest in it, need for it, means of sharing it, and discussion about it online. I don't think demand is the problem. Business models most certainly are a problem (though to say that business models are the only problem is to fool ourselves into thinking that the rest of journalism needn't change). So I will concentrate in the third part of this essay on possible new models, including some we have been studying at the Tow-Knight Center for Entrepreneurial Journalism, which I direct at the City University of New York's Graduate

School of Journalism. The goal is to find sustainable — that is, profitable — support for news. But that is not merely a discussion of replacing lost revenue; we also must examine new efficiencies in what will surely be smaller, post-monopoly news enterprises. Mostly, we must concentrate on where and how journalism adds value to a community's knowledge and only then consider how it can extract value for its sustenance. So perhaps the news industry must think past the idea that it is in the content, advertising, and distribution businesses. Perhaps we should ask whether — like Google and Facebook — news instead should be a service that helps people accomplish their goals. Here I return to the relationship strategy for news and explore the opportunity to build new business models around value over volume.

I ask us to question nearly every assumption about news but by no means to reject them all. In the face of disruption, we need to reaffirm and preserve established values. At CUNY, our founding dean, Steve Shepard, emphasizes that we must teach the eternal verities of journalism, including accuracy, fairness, and completeness. Here I will argue that the key question journalists must ask today is how they add value to the flow of information in a community, a flow that can now occur without mediators — that is, without media. Journalists will continue to do that by trying to answer the questions that aren't being asked, adding reporting and often using narrative to provide the sense and context that is all the more needed today. As journalists concentrate on where they can bring real value instead of their old production ethos — manufacturing newspapers, magazines, and TV shows — they can rise above the commodification and devaluation of their trade.

I start this exercise using a broad (some may say too broad) definition of journalism, which is: helping a community better organize its knowledge so it can better organize itself. Journalism has always endeavored to do that. But we in the field came to define ourselves less by our value and mission and more by our media and tools — ink on pulp or slick paper, sound or images over airwaves. Now we have new tools to exploit. Those tools require new skills and create new value. But at the core, we serve citizens and communities. As this essay progresses, I will expand and contract that definition of journalism like an accordion. I will narrow it drastically when I seek to identify the essence of journalism, its greatest value and service, that which we must preserve in this time of economic turmoil in the industry. I will broaden the definition when I describe inclusive news ecosystems that can serve many communities, many interests, and many needs and that can band together in networks that can share content, audience, technology, support, and, I hope, advertising sales.

We have much to emulate from the inventors of the net: Vint Cerf's and his colleagues' creation of standards and protocols that enforce the principle of enabling anyone to speak with anyone;[10] Sir Tim Berners-Lee's implementation of the simple link to connect people and information; Google's quest to organize and make accessible the world's information (not to mention reinvent advertising); Wikipedia's similar goal (without the advertising); Mark Zuckerberg's creation of a platform to connect people; the creation of platforms by Blogger, WordPress, and Movable Type that enable anyone to create and share what they have to say; Twitter surprising itself to become a tool for instantly updating the world — with news; Tumblr's and Pinterest's insight in making interest the engine of distribution; YouTube for making content embeddable everywhere; Reddit for attempting to channel the energy that fuels comments into collaboration; Kickstarter, Indiegogo and now Beacon Readers for harnessing the generosity of crowds; Amazon for building platforms and learning from the signals we generate to serve us with greater relevance.

We also can learn much from these innovators' instinct to experiment and shift direction (pivot, as they say) and their willingness, even eagerness, to learn and fail. These are geeks' gifts.

We need to look for the opportunities that technology and its disruption bring. I hope that every reader of this essay outdoes me, finding more and better routes to explore — and exploring them. I hope to hear the discussion about news shift from its lost past to its future — its many possible futures.

PART 1: RELATIONSHIPS

NO MAS MASS MEDIA

"There are in fact no masses," said sociologist Raymond Williams, "there are only ways of seeing people as masses."[11] Without masses, what then of mass media? Media are built to serve people at scale, all at once, all the same. Our industrial wonder is that we could even accomplish that, manufacturing and distributing a complex and timely product in print or harnessing technology to reach untold millions via broadcast every single day. Our organizations and business models are built for bulk. We are invested in the masses. Hell, media invented mass.

I still hear people my age lament the passing of the Cronkite era's grand shared experience of media, as if we all were meant to sit at the same time watching the same images of the same news. That was a short-lived era indeed, from the mid-'50s — when the arrival of television killed the diversity of voices from competitive newspapers in most American cities, leaving the lone survivors to serve everyone the same — to the mid-'90s and the arrival of the internet, which mortally wounded those monopolistic newspapers and threatened TV's media hegemony. But the net's real victim was not one medium or another. What it killed was the idea of the mass.

Should we continue to serve people as a mass now that we can serve and connect them as individuals? I will argue throughout this essay that relationships — knowing people as individuals and communities so we can better serve them with more relevance, building greater value as a result — will be a necessity for media business models, a key to survival and success. Yes, of course, we will still make content. But content is not the end product. It is only one tool we will use to inform and serve our communities and their members. Content may still have intrinsic value as something to sell. But now it also has value as a means to learn about a person: what she is interested in, what she knows and wants to know, where she lives, what she does — all signals that can enable a news organization to deliver her greater value and earn more loyalty, engagement, and revenue in turn. That is how Google, Facebook, and Amazon operate.

Unfortunately, we in news are not built to do that. Offline, we may have readers' names on subscription lists, along with their addresses and credit card numbers to bill and deliver to them. Online, even if we have collected their email addresses or demanded they register by name, we still don't have the means to gather, understand, and serve their individual needs and interests. We don't know them. We count them. We still want these anonymous "unique users" to add up to a critical mass so we can serve them "pageviews" and sell them to advertisers en masse. Those are the mass-media metrics by which we still measure success.

I know of more than one local news site that worked so hard to perfect their search-engine optimization that they ended up attracting millions of users and pageviews from outside their markets. Those users are worthless to the local advertisers that provide almost all the revenue for these sites. These out-of-market users either wreck the performance of local ads — who wants to click on a sale a thousand miles away? — or are served low-value network or remnant advertising. I asked these sites to calculate the value of in-market vs. out-of-market users and they found the former worth at least 20 times the latter. So there is the first cinder block in building a relationship with a user: Does she live in your market? That's not big data. It's small data. Next, a news organization should want to learn where she lives and works so it can give her news around her home and restaurant reviews near her office. More small data. Then it may want to learn this person's interests, gender, age, and marital and parental status. She won't tell us these things simply because we want her to or require her to — how often have you lied on a pesky registration form? She will reveal herself to us only if she benefits in return, if she engages in a voluntary transaction built on mutual value. If we want to learn where a person lives and works, why not for example build a traffic and transit information service that helps with her daily commute? That may not come in the form of content as we know it: articles in inverted pyramids. Instead it should bring her functionality such as embedded maps from Google or Waze, travel schedules with the means for commuters to fact-check them, and a platform allowing commuters as a community to share tips, frustrations, and warnings about their shared routes to work. See, for example, CleverCommute.com.

Once we do know more about her, we can give her more relevant service as well as more relevant advertising or commerce, wasting less of her time on content she doesn't care about and wasting fewer merchants' dollars pitching a restaurant two hours away or trying to sell a stroller to a grandparent. The content and services we give to this person will still, of course, need to include news we believe everyone will want to know — about the governor's race or the big storm coming — but overall the content should progressively and effortlessly become smarter about the person: personalized by giving priority to news about her town or her children's school or her interest in tennis and the company where she works.

Media people must learn key relationship skills: how to provide services that give people a reason to reveal themselves; how to build their trust so they will do that; how to gather this data; how to analyze it; how to act on it for for the good of the users; and how to exploit it for economic benefit. It's critical that we deliver value before extracting it. That is what Google does by giving away free services such as its Mail, Maps, Calendar, Drive, Docs, Plus, Hangouts, and YouTube. And that is why Google has entered into new businesses beyond search, especially mobile. Each of these services generates signals about people that Google can act on to provide relevance and value for users and in turn build untold value for Google. Using Google Maps on my Android phone, I gladly tell Google where I am and where I'm going so Google can help get me there. Thus Google knows where I live and work but my local newspaper doesn't. I tell Google what I'm looking for so it can help me find it. I tell Google who my friends are in case they have any recommendations. I'm not violating my privacy and neither is Google. I'm choosing to do this. I'm gaining benefit in a relationship built on information, service, and trust. (Doesn't that sound like the basis of a new mission for news media?)

The next frontier for Google as well as Amazon and countless other companies, from credit-card issuers to coupon services, is to get closer to our transactions. That will offer the most valuable data of all, and is one reason Google and Amazon are experimenting with same-day delivery of goods bought online, pitting them against many of the local retailers who are newspapers' advertisers (there's another brick pulled out of our Jenga tower). They are all fighting to know who we are, where we are, and what we want. They are trying to find ways to help us get it. These skills will be key to resurrecting at least newspapers (that is, local media companies) and magazines (that is, interest-based media companies) and perhaps broadcast (the most mass of mass media).

A local online news site should know where you live and what you care about. It should have more opportunities to learn more about you than a gigantic, global company such as Google, because it can help inform you about your town (and thus learn where you live and perhaps which issues there matter to you); it can help you find good places to eat through your neighbors' recommendations (and so find out you're vegetarian); it can help you amuse yourself (and learn what sports you follow and what kind of music and movies you like); it can connect you with people in a community (and discover, for example, whether you are a parent or a wrestling fan). News organizations can use this information to personalize the delivery of what they already make — that's the easy part — but also should use it to inform their priorities and how they use their resources in building services. At About.com, where I consulted when The New York Times bought it, writers studied the search queries that brought readers to their site. If people were asking questions for which About.com didn't have ready answers, the staff wrote the answers. Witnessing that was a °duh° moment for me. Shouldn't all news organizations have robust means to listen to the needs and curiosities of the public? Now, some journalists will say that their work should not be dictated by public desires or else we'll feed people nothing but . . . well, nothing but the gossip and gore we already feed them in abundance. There is nothing wrong with listening to the people we serve. If you discover there are thousands of cancer patients in your market, then why not add an oncologist's blog and a cancer community? If you learn that people are enraged about train service, that's the best reason to assign a reporter to investigate.

Relationship skills could be even more important to magazines. Some years ago, I was asked to be on a panel at a magazine industry conference. A few days before the event, its organizer called me and asked, "Uh, Jeff, are you going to say that magazines are doomed?" Before I could answer, he added: "And if you are, could you please not come?" So I asked myself whether magazines have cause for hope. I decided they should be able to make the transition to online because magazines already were surrounded by communities of shared interest and information — and the net serves communities well. But these days, it looks as if I may have been wrong. Gourmet, Mademoiselle, and Parenting are dead. So many titles are shrunken and suffering. The once-vaunted Time Inc., object of desire first for Warner Bros. and then AOL, was exiled from Time Warner to keep its bad karma away from the entertainment empire. I used to love magazines. I bought them by the pound. I worked for them. I started one, Entertainment Weekly. But I don't buy them now, in print or on my tablet. Like magazine queen Tina Brown, I don't even read them much anymore.[12] Yet I'm not giving up on magazines, just as I'm not giving up on newspapers. They both still have so much potential to convene people around an interest or an idea and to serve and bring value to communities and their members.

As we in media build new skills around relationships, we must first stop seeing people as a mass. We need to know them, then serve them as individuals and communities. And so, as I will further explore in the third part of this essay, we need to shift our metrics of success from anonymous mass measurements — circulation, unique users, pageviews, email addresses — to metrics of relationships:

- How many people do we know (even if not by name but merely by location, need, interest, or behavior)?
- How many reasons do we give these people to let us know more about them (what relevant services do we offer)?
- How much do we know about each individual — how many small data points about each person have we gathered?
- How are we able to exploit that information for their benefit?
- How can we exploit this information for our benefit — through advertising, fees, data, events, or other models (which I'll explore in the last part of this essay)?

- What communities exist among our users (for just as they are not a mass, they are not a single public, a single community)?
- And a very important metric for journalism: How informed are members of our community? As informed as they want to be? That requires that we first ask people and listen to them about their needs and the outcomes they desire and *then* find the best means to fulfill those needs: through platforms that enable them to share, through education, through data made open, and through reporting and narrative. This leads to our most critical measurement of journalistic value: Did the people we serve accomplish their goals?

CONTENT VS. SERVICE

Is news really a content business? Should it be? Perhaps defining ourselves as content creators is a trap. That worldview convinces us that our value is embodied entirely in what we make rather than in the good people derive from it. The belief that our business is to produce a product called content is what drives us to build paywalls around it — to argue that the public *should* pay for what we make because it costs us money to make it and, besides, they've always paid for it. It motivates us to fight over protecting our content from what we view as theft — using copyright — rather than recognizing the value that content and the information in it can bring in informing relationships. As content creators, we separate ourselves from the public while we create our product until we are finished and make it public — because that is what our means of production and distribution long demanded; only now are we learning to collaborate during the process. Our monopoly over those means of production also convinced us that we could own, control, and wield pricing power over this scarcity called content.

These circumstances left us ill-prepared for a technological era when copies cost nothing; when content and thus competition are abundant; when information becomes a commodity the instant it can be passed on with a link and click; and when the value of information — before it is spread and known — has a half-life now measured in milliseconds. Content, it turns out, is not a great business.

To suggest that we are not in the content business is to argue that journalists are not primarily storytellers: high heresy indeed. That idea pulls the rug out from under everything we assume and hold dear about our craft and trade: our job descriptions, our production processes, our legal status, our measures of success, and certainly our business models. Fear not: Content will continue to be valued. But content's value may be more as a tool than as an end in itself and certainly not as our only product.

Well then, if we are not in the content business, what business are we in? Consider journalism as a service. Content is that which fills something. Service is that which accomplishes something. To be a service, news must be concerned with outcomes rather than products. What should journalism's result be? That seems obvious: better-informed individuals and a better-informed society. But who's to define "informed" and who's to measure success: journalists or citizens? Jay Rosen challenged me on Twitter, saying that if journalism is a service then it must have terms of service. Shouldn't it be the public that sets those terms?

Journalists have believed that informing the public is their job and that the role of editors is to decide what the public ought to know. We set the terms of service. We define what it means to be an informed citizen. We often complain as well that too much of society is ill-informed. Let's put aside that rather paternalistic attitude toward the public we serve. If we do not believe in the will of the public to be informed, then we might as well give up on democracy, free markets, and the ideals of education, not to mention journalism. I am confident that there will continue to be a market demand for the information a society needs to function. That must be an article of faith if we are to hold out hope to sustain journalism.

Let's also acknowledge that, in the oft-quoted and misquoted words of Dan Gillmor, our public knows more than we do.[13] So our job isn't only to inform the public. It is also our job to help them inform each other. In the past, when somebody knew what others needed to know, we had limited tools to spread that knowledge: a reporter found the expert, witness, or official to answer a question and the news organization distributed what she learned. Now we have more tools at hand that allow communities to communicate directly. So perhaps our first task in expanding journalism's service should be to offer platforms that help individuals and communities to seek, reveal, gather, share, organize, analyze, understand, and use their own information — or to better use the platforms that already exist, from Twitter to Facebook to Reddit. The internet has proven to be good at helping communities inform themselves, sharing what's happening via Twitter, what's known via Wikipedia, and what matters to people through conversational tools. Comments, blog posts, and tweets — nevermind their frequent banality and repetition and sometimes incivility — tap the cultural consciousness.

Of course, there is much that a community needs to know that is not in that exchange of information. That is where journalists can and should add to a community's knowledge by asking questions that are not already answered — by reporting and investigating; by adding context and explanation; by finding and including expertise in the discussion; by weighing trust and authority; by checking facts and debunking assumptions and rumors; by making information accessible through narrative or visualization; and by packaging and presenting through editing, curation, and discovery. Most of those skills are old: what journalists have long done, only now made faster. Some skills are new, facilitated by technology: presenting data for the public to interrogate; making tools; convening discussion; organizing activities. So, yes, there is a need for journalists. But simply distribut-ing information is no longer our monopoly as gatekeepers and no longer a proper use of our scarce resources. Without that monopoly on information, we can no longer claim that it is up to us to decide what the public should know. People can more easily find out what they need to know without us. Indeed, the more we help them do that on their own, the better: The public is better informed; journalists have more opportunities to add their value; and the entire enterprise of news costs less.

This idea of outcomes-oriented journalism requires that we respect the public and what it knows and needs and wants to know. It forces us to stop thinking that we know better than the public. It leads us to create systems to gather the public's knowledge. Recall that this was the key insight that led Larry Page and Sergey Brin to invent Google's search and business: They trusted the clicks of the users. They created a system to observe and learn from those clicks, using that data to help them organize the world's knowledge and make it accessible and relevant to every user as an individual. Doesn't that also sound like a restatement of journalism's true mission?

Let me apply these ideas to a practical example: In 2012, when Hurricane Sandy struck New Jersey, where I live, and New York, where I work, my information needs were clear: I wanted to know which streets were closed, where power was out, where power crews were working, what gas stations were open and stocked, what stores and restaurants were open (and had wi-fi), and which transit lines were operating. Most of that information — that data — is best presented in constantly updated lists. But news media mostly gave me articles, which only summarized that data and guaranteed its incompleteness as well as its staleness and eventual inaccuracy. Narratives informing me that a lot of trees had fallen and many homes were without power — salted with quotes from fellow residents — told me nothing I didn't already know and nothing I needed. The shortcomings of the article are a necessary condition of our prior means of production and the business model that resulted. We needed to package information into the confines of pages or shows — thus, stories. We could afford only so many reporters and they had only so many ways to gather information directly, so our knowledge was necessarily incomplete. Those conditions no longer apply. We have new ways to gather more information from more sources and to make it available to individuals as they need it. And we have the means to find out what they need.

Imagine if a local news site had put up a simple map allowing residents in town to post pictures of their streets and neighborhoods with captions — metadata — telling us which streets were closed and where power crews were working, with time used as a factor in displaying relevance. The site needn't have built that map. It could have employed functionality from Google Maps, SeeClickFix (a service that lets neighbors report problems around them), or Ushahidi (an open-source platform to collect and present information on maps). And then the local media organization could have used its power to convene the community's attention and urge neighbors to share more information. Working in networks with local bloggers, the editors could have combined the knowledge of many audiences, many communities. The news site's reporters could have contributed more data, obtaining information from the power company and local government about where they said their crews were working — and then asking residents to confirm the truth of authorities' assertions. (This is an example of journalistic skepticism and follow-through that was sadly missing in coverage in my town.) By providing the means for residents and officials to share data, the news organization can effectively and efficiently check off many of my information needs.

Where there's a checkmark missing, *that* is where reporting is needed. That is when the journalist challenges the utility over its inaccurate dispatches or calls the schools superintendent to ask what her requirements will be for reopening. The journalist can ask the people in town what else they need to know. If the platform that the news site provides is flexible enough, then users will take it over to meet their own, unpredictable needs (such flexibility is a necessary criterion of a true platform). My neighbors with generators could have posted offers to let others charge their phones, and neighbors without generators could have banded together to buy them before the next storm (allowing savvy electricians to see the discussion and bid for the business).

This worldview resets the essential relationship of the journalist to the public. It says the public knows more than the journalist. It makes it possible for the journalist to listen to the public's needs. It not only creates a collaborative relationship between journalist and public, it puts the journalist in the proper role as servant to the public, following its lead. This is more than crowdsourcing — that is, sharing work with the public, asking them to complete the jobs that journalists already do. This arrangement allows the public to use tools as it sees fit to share the information it wants to share. That is a way of envisioning journalism as a service, not as content.

If we see content as a tool in the service of journalism and of our communities — rather than as an end and as the essence of our business — then we change more than our relationship with the public. We change our processes: We listen first and open channels to do so. We build systems that help a community to share what it already knows — the more the better — and we monitor that flow of information and conversation to see where our skills are needed to anoint authority, eliminate repetition, correct errors, improve presentation, fill in blanks. We change our job descriptions: I'm not suggesting that journalists all become coders, the better to build platforms. But we should begin to see ourselves as enablers, sometimes educators, even organizers and, yes advocates. We change how we measure our success — on the number, depth, quality, and value of the relationships we build — and how well-informed and well-equipped people are as a result. Perhaps we reconsider even our defensiveness over copyright, if we are no longer the exclusive creators of all news content but also are redistributors of others' information. And that, of course, depends on whether we manage to change our business models (which I discuss in the third part of this essay), building value in relationships rather than in merely manufacturing a commodity: content. Once again, that is Google's, Facebook's, Amazon's, and eBay's bet: that knowing and then anticipating individuals' needs will generate value, whether through fees or advertising or commerce.

I had lunch sometime ago with a former TV news executive who complained that Google and Facebook use media's steel to make their cars — that is, that they commoditize content, using it to extract greater profit from their high end of the value chain. "Mark Zuckerberg," he said, "does not respect content." I thought about that for a moment and disagreed. "No," I said, "I think Zuckerberg respects content more than we do. We respect only the content we make. If content people don't make it, it's not content, it's junk." But Mark Zuckerberg finds value in that supposed junk, as does Larry Page. They recognize that the content the public creates in its sharing and conversation online can generate signals about both the information and the individuals: Who they are, where they are, where they're going, where they've been, whom they know, what they know, what they want to know, what they want, what they like, what they buy. All those signals enable those companies to target content, services, sales, and advertising to users, giving the users relevance and treating them as individuals and not merely as members of a demographic.

I told this executive a story I'd written in *What Would Google Do?* about seeing Zuckerberg questioned by a powerful media executive at the World Economic Forum annual meeting in Davos.[14] "Mark," the executive implored, "tell me how to make a community.

We should be able to own communities. Tell me how." Zuckerberg, a geek of few words, answered with two: "You can't." Full stop. After an uncomfortable pause, he told this room full of media executives that they were asking the wrong question. "You don't make communities," he said. "Communities already exist. They're already doing what they want to do. The question you should be asking is how you can help them do what they want to do better." His prescription for them was to bring communities "elegant organization." That's what young Mark did for Harvard and then the rest of us. That's what journalism has long attempted to do, and that is how I came to the definition of journalism I shared in the introduction: helping communities organize their knowledge so they can better organize themselves. Now we have many more and some better ways to do that.

If our role as journalists is to help communities better organize their knowledge and themselves, then it is apparent that we are in the service business and that we must draw on many tools, including content, and place value on the relationships we build with members of our communities. We are in the relationship business. So now let us begin to catalog the forms those relationships can take with the people we serve, with the ecosystems in which we work, and with our business partners.

NEWS AS PLATFORM

Back to Hurricane Sandy. When news sites all-in-all failed to give me the information I needed or the means to get it, I used other tools to turn directly to my neighbors. I went to Patch, the hyperlocal news service then owned by Aol. Patch was one of the news services that gave me articles with stale summaries of too little information. But it also provided a blogging platform that allowed me to publish a brief screed complaining that our town was spreading misinformation by distributing a list of streets where the power company was supposedly working — including ones around me, where nary a truck was to be seen. I criticized the town for taking the utility at its unreliable word. In the comments under that post, other residents joined in, checked the list against their streets, and shared their observations and my frustration. It was through collaboration with my fellow townspeople — not a reporter's reporting — that we could fact-check the utility's list. If only a local news organization had provided that functionality with a more organized platform, better than comments, to let us to share what we knew. It could have posted the list in a wiki where we could add notations or to a map where we could add pictures and reports.

My neighbors and I got our chainsaws out to remove about three dozen trees from our street and driveways just so we could get out and so emergency crews could get in. We were all without power. Once freed, some neighbors went to stay elsewhere — my family, luckily, in a hotel; others with relatives or at vacation homes. The neighborhood Sandy diaspora wanted to stay in touch to stay informed. We resorted first to email but the chain became unwieldy. So I opened an account at a new service, Nextdoor, which promised a private network for neighbors with verified addresses. There was a platform! I hit a few snags: Nextdoor's address database was missing many of my neighbors' home addresses and wouldn't let me correct it. The service insisted that I include a minimum of 75 homes in my neighborhood even though, in my semi-rural area, that meant including people I'd never met who lived more than two miles away. And it prescribed topics for discussion — crime and safety, primarily — instead of what we really wanted to talk about: getting power back on or, later, buying generators. A true platform would have allowed users to best define how to use it. So we reverted to inefficient email. In the meantime, I've met Nextdoor's founder, Nirav Tolia, who raised $100 million from an impressive set of investors: Kleiner Perkins, Greylock Partners, Benchmark, Jeff Bezos' personal fund, Google Ventures, Allen & Co. The company is addressing these issues and building a promising platform for neighbors to connect and share information in a private, trusted environment. I've spoken with him about how local media should be involved. Tolia says Nextdoor can exist because Facebook blew its chance to create a platform for verified identity. I'd add that Nextdoor can exist because local newspapers missed the opportunity to be Nextdoor.

After the hurricane, New Jersey suffered a gasoline shortage, because downed trees and flooding blocked deliveries and service stations lost power. When stations did open up, lines formed for miles, so police had to come and direct traffic. The police knew when stations had power and gas and would be open. They could have shared that information with the public, and media could have helped them do that. But they didn't. So drivers sought any tool that could help while wasting precious gas driving around looking for more of it. Many resorted to another rather unwieldy platform: Twitter, where we shared information around the hashtag #njgas. It was an imperfect system, because it meant reading alerts about open stations too many miles away and because the information had a very short shelf life. Still, it was the best available information and it was useful enough to tell me to head west, toward Pennsylvania, where I would find fuel. In gratitude, I contributed my own updates about open stations.

What if a local news organization provided a platform that could have met our needs post-Sandy — or on any day? What would that look like? I don't mean that it should build another Twitter or Nextdoor. Note well that in the case of Twitter, the real platform wasn't so much the technology but the social convention of the hashtag. The idea of the hashtag itself was first proposed by Chris Messina, not an employee of Twitter, who suggested in 2007 that it would be a way to find tweets around events or topics.[15] NJ.com claimed credit for starting and promoting the specific #njgas hashtag after Sandy. Platforms need not be made via coding. They can often be made via common, spontaneous conventions. News organizations have the megaphone to help establish those conventions.

There are many ways a news organization can become a platform. It can provide existing technology (wikis, forums, maps, data bases, surveys, and more) and work through existing services its communities already use (culling relevant information and reports from YouTube, Twitter, Facebook, Tumblr, Google+, Pinterest, Vine, Tout, et al). News organizations can explore new technologies (for example, sensors that report the environment around them, wearable cameras, video streaming from phones, data analysis of social conversation) to facilitate the sharing of information. It can also help independent bloggers and community correspondents succeed at covering their own towns — offering them content, promotion, technology, advertising networks, training, and the means to collaborate. News organizations no longer operate alone, in monopolies or silos. They live surrounded by many competitors or collaborators — how you view them depends on your worldview — in a disorganized but growing ecosystem of news.

ECOSYSTEMS
AND NETWORKS

After the invention of the high-speed press, news became a vertically organized industry. Single corporations controlled every step: the entire process of defining, reporting, and producing news; its manufacture, its distribution, its sale, and its support through advertising sales. In the last half of the last century, especially in America, news companies operated in oligopolies or often as monopolies. They maintained pricing power over the cost of content to consumers and advertising to sponsors. They wielded buying power over suppliers. The arrangement was great — for publishers, at least — while it lasted. It's no wonder those news companies mourn its passing. The single force that powered their empires was scarcity: control over the precious resources of production and distribution.

Now, of course, we all hold the means of production and distribution for news, information, and content in our hands with our keyboards or phones (or whatever devices follow). Anyone can gather and distribute information; anyone can find or join an appropriate public; everyone can be connected to anyone without need of gatekeepers or mediators — that is, media. Abundance rules in digital. As publishers shrink, they may claim that news is becoming scarcer because *they* make less of it. But in truth news is growing — albeit unevenly and in many ways unreliably — via no end of new sources contributing to a larger information ecosystem.

Let's examine my home state, New Jersey, as an example of a news ecosystem. We've never really had a television station to call our own; instead New York and Philadelphia beam over the border to us. Our little-watched public TV station was handed over by the state to New York's PBS station, WNET. Our little-heard public radio stations were also taken over by stations in New York and Philadelphia, WNYC and WHYY respectively. Our one notable statewide radio station, NJ101.5, is — how shall I put this with academic rigor and grace? — dreck. We have one once-dominant newspaper, The Star-Ledger, owned by Advance Publications (where I used to work and still advise), and its affiliated news service, NJ.com. There are a few more dailies owned by Gannett and local families, and a slew of weeklies. They all are shrinking. The New York Times used to cover New Jersey but has all but given up to pursue international ambitions. The Philadelphia Inquirer is holding on for dear life. Such is the state of legacy media in New Jersey.

But we do have a growing cadre of local bloggers such as Baristanet in Montclair, Red Bank Green, My Verona NJ, Cliffview Pilot, Elizabeth Inside Out (published by a former CUNY entrepreneurial student, serving a town poorer than the rest), Brick City Live (from another CUNY student, serving Newark), Morristown Green (another CUNYite), Rahway Rising (writing just about redevelopment), The Alternative Press (which covers a handful of towns), and a few dozen more. But I wish for many more than that. We have local communities such as Jersey Shore Hurricane News connecting through Facebook (from yet another CUNY veteran), where thousands of people gathered to share information during two big storms and continue to connect. Neighbors in Maplewood and South Orange still get together in a bulletin board at Maplewood Online. Cranford Radio covers its town in audio. We have what's left of Aol's Patch. Nextdoor is growing. Former newspaper people are managing to eke out a living and continue their beat reporting at NJ Spotlight and New Jersey Newsroom. The New York Observer runs the web site PolitickerNJ, a mini Politico for Trenton; its core business is selling a premium newsletter with gavel-to-gavel statehouse coverage called State Street Wire. There are sites serving special interests: Glocally Newark covers culture in the city; Barista Kids serves moms in Montclair; Pharmalot covers the state's international pharmaceutical industry (it was started inside the Star-Ledger, then run independently by its author, then absorbed into the Wall Street Journal); Jersey Bites reviews restaurants, as do a few other blogs; Clever Commute offers services to long-suffering commuters, including a $35-a-year premium app. Not-for-profit investigative news organization ProPublica does much work in the state. Independent public radio station WBGO is a worldwide jazz brand and WFMU is so independent it's impossible to describe; each has convened international audiences online. There's robust but isolated ethnic media in the state. And there's the appropriately named WeirdNJ, which compiles our many oddities. Finally, let's not forget the thousands upon thousands of New Jerseyans who share information with each other on Twitter, Facebook, Pinterest, Tumblr, forums on NJ.com and other media sites, and via their own blogs. When I use the words "news organization," I could mean any of them, not just the big, old newspaper.

There are many nonmedia contributors to the New Jersey ecosystem. State agencies and local governments are slowly getting better at sharing their information, adding to the ecosystem. The Town Stats Project is a humble effort to begin to collate local data. Companies such as utilities share information in spurts. Google obviously offers much information, from traffic to weather to restaurants to news aggregation. Google also delivers audience and, in some cases, revenue (though not much) to sites in the state. Facebook provides audience and in one case — the Jersey Shore Hurricane News — a platform for publishing and for finding collaborators to contribute news. Twitter provides promotion as well as tips and content — ditto Instagram and YouTube. WordPress is the most commonly used publishing system. Apple and Android enable some services to make and sell apps. And I hope someone — an existing participant or someone new — will build an advertising network that can aggregate the audience of many of these sites to reach the critical mass needed to sell to larger, state-wide marketers. (I'm working on that.)

You get the idea. New Jersey — like many markets — now has a growing and disorganized hodgepodge of sites, services, communities, and individuals operating on various platforms with different motives, with more or fewer resources, and with business models from none to not-for-profit to hoping-for-profit to profitable. They all contribute to a larger ecosystem of information in the state and its communities.

This notion of an ecosystem can be confusing as we leave an era dominated by monolithic media — large, vertically integrated companies with tangible products, obvious control over scarce resources, and clear brands. Now we have this untidy hydra we call an ecosystem. No one is in charge. It has huge blank spots — there are 565 towns in New Jersey, each an opportunity for corruption needing a watchdog, and only a few dozen of them covered. There is no longer a single, simple business model: circulation + advertising. Quality and credibility are sometimes question marks. Surely, you say, this is not an improvement. Perhaps not yet, but it can be. My state is a blank slate where innovation and collaboration can bloom, where more voices than ever can be heard, where citizens can end up better informed and more engaged than they were. But to get there, the ecosystem needs help and its members need to help each other. Members of an ecosystem can share content, audience, and best practices. They can share effort on collaborative projects, accomplishing more together than they could alone. They can share revenue through joint advertising sales and other activities, like events. They can also save on expenses by pooling their purchasing power for space, technology, or services. Later, when I explore new efficiencies for news, I will examine the impact of the link on a news ecosystem: how it forces each member to specialize and concentrate on what it does best and how it enables every member of an ecosystem to link to its complementary colleagues. Members of an ecosystem eventually learn a Golden Rule of linking: Linking to others is a service to readers and a courtesy to the site that receives the link. Linking can and should be a virtuous circle.

None of this will happen on its own. Lone-wolf journalists and monopolistic publishers are among the least likely professionals to think collaboratively. In the early days of the commercial web, more than a dozen large American newspaper publishers banded together to create the New Century Network, which was supposed to help them share content, audience, and advertising sales and build market power against the growing, frightening power of Prodigy and Yahoo. The Silicon Valley venture-capital firm Kleiner Perkins thought the network was such a good idea that it wanted to invest. But the newspapers could not agree even to take the money. Instead, the newspapers wasted their own money. In the end, which came quickly, the network died. News organizations must learn that it is in their enlightened self-interest to reach out and cooperate within the ecosystems that now surround them. Collaboration is an imperative for survival.

To lead horses to water in New Jersey and create a structure to foster and support collaboration in the state's news ecosystem, I have had the privilege of working with Chris Daggett and Molly de Aguiar at the Geraldine R. Dodge Foundation, the John S. and James

L. Knight Foundation, and other philanthropies to help develop a New Jersey model for a collaborative news ecosystem. A first building block of the project was to open the New Jersey News Commons at Montclair State University. It was started by the cofounder of Baristanet, Debbie Galant, whom I'd crowned the queen of hyperlocal. The Commons was assigned four tasks:

- To train members of the ecosystem in the skills of journalism, media, and business.
- To curate, distribute, and thus encourage the best work from the ecosystem across its members. The Commons set up a network that allows members to embed each others' articles and posts on any of their sites; later I'll explain that in greater depth.
- To foster collaboration among members of the ecosystem.
- To provide services members of the ecosystem need. We hope that could include libel and health insurance, though they are difficult to come by.

These sites also need business support — to improve advertising sales and develop other revenue streams, such as events — which is coming from the Local News Lab at the Dodge Foundation, run by de Aguiar and Josh Stearns. At first, we thought it was important for Montclair State to provide space so members of the ecosystem — public TV, public radio, NJ Spotlight, NJ.com, bloggers, and technology providers — could work alongside each other. But that turned out to be much less important than other mechanisms for collaboration. So far, members of the ecosystem have joined in a content- and audience-sharing network, learned how to share information on election nights, worked on collaborative reporting projects around Hurricane Sandy recovery and immigration, shared best practices with each other, and taken training in a wide range of topics.

At the same time at CUNY, colleagues Sarah Bartlett and Garry Pierre-Pierre created a Center for Community and Ethnic Media, where they also provide training and translate the work of various publications into English so it can be shared and reach a wider audience. They are helping the New Jersey News Commons reach out to ethnic publications throughout the state. At the Center for Entrepreneurial Journalism, we have undertaken business research to benefit all these entities. In research on the state of the New Jersey ecosystem overseen by my CUNY colleague Chris Anderson, he concluded that networks are necessary for the survival and success of members of the ecosystem — but networks need leaders. Those leaders can be strong-willed members of the ecosystem. They can be foundations or universities. These leaders should also include large, old-media companies that can find new life, new growth, new audiences, and new efficiency by bringing together members of their news ecosystems into formal networks.

There's one big issue with trying to forge a network out of the emerging ecosystem in a market like New Jersey: There aren't enough nodes yet to make a fully functioning network. In other words, the ecosystem isn't big enough; it needs more members to cover more communities. That leads to a new and necessary role for incumbent members of the ecosystems: incubation. The Commons has administered small start-up grants for new sites, but we still need to do much more to encourage new journalists and community members to start their own beat businesses. We need to grow the ecosystem. It is in the enlightened self-interest of the existing entities to encourage, recruit, train, and support new colleagues in the ecosystem. The more nodes in the network, the more valuable the network is for all. The more hyperlocal blogs there are to report on towns in the market, the less reporting large news organizations need to do, the more news they have to point to, and the more these news organizations can concentrate on large-scale reporting and investigations. The larger the ecosystem, the more outlets there are to distribute other members' content. The larger the ecosystem, the larger the audience that can be delivered to major advertisers that still want to reach an entire market. On and on the list of benefits goes.

Incumbent members of news ecosystems should actively recruit, train, mentor, and support new members. When a newspaper lays off journalists — as happens too often and will continue until news organizations reach their sustainable sizes — why not offer to help these experienced and trusted professionals set up new businesses? Give them a technology platform and assured distribution as well as a base of advertising income until they reach critical mass. Foundations can look at critical areas of coverage that are missing in a market. They can issue challenges to find entrepreneurially inclined journalists to fill those needs, helping them with seed funding and training. Networks can recruit and train people to fill blank spots in coverage. The New Jersey News Commons did just that by recruiting news bloggers in communities ravaged by Hurricane Sandy and giving them seed grants and training, funded by Dodge and Knight. Universities can train journalists in the business skills they lack. They can train local entrepreneurs in journalism and skills that may be new to them. The goal: A larger, better, more effective and sustainable news ecosystem serving a community.

ENGAGEMENT, COLLABORATION, AND MEMBERSHIP

One of the greatest crises facing news organizations — well, besides disrupted business models, unlimited competition, and eroding trust — is engagement. The indications are pitiful: News accounts for only 6.7 percent of site visits on the internet, 1.3 percent of time spent, and 0.9 percent of pages viewed, according to the newspaper trade association WAN/IFRA. In 2012, the group said, digital engagement was 5 percent of print's — is it a coincidence that digital revenues were also 5 percent of those in print? At CUNY, our research on new business models for news found that news sites typically garnered a dozen pageviews per user per month. Facebook gets that much engagement from members *every day*. Consider, too, that when The New York Times put up its pay meter, it allowed 20 free pageviews per month but then dropped that number by half to increase the number of people who would even see a demand for pay. Those readers — a fraction of the total — are considered "loyal." Thus the vast majority of Times readers see fewer than 10 pages per month — and that is for the best journalism has to offer.

Mind you, these are the most superficial of measurements of engagement: how many people are merely looking at a page of content that we create, and how long they spend doing so. Reach, frequency, unique users, pageviews, shares, likes, attention — these are all measures centered on us and our product, content, rather than on the people we serve. In mass-media economics, more is always better: more people coming more often to spend more time on our content. Pew's Andrew Kohut has worried — as I just have — about declining time spent with news, particularly among young people. "Younger generations just don't enjoy following news," he wrote.[16] But as I thought about his complaint, I started to wonder whether less time spent with news is necessarily a bad thing. Perhaps young people are more efficient in getting the news they need than their elders, who still stare at TV screens for an hour to get a few minutes' worth of information. In any event, our old definitions of engagement are insufficient. There are now so many better and richer means of engaging with those we serve in our communities. Let us consider a range of possibilities.

Acquaintance: Start with just knowing someone or knowing something about him or her. Return to the earlier discussion of small data: Is there sufficient trust and good reason for a person to identify herself — who she is, where she lives, where she works, what she likes to do, what her interests are, whether she has children, and so on? Nevermind how many "unique users" you have. How many people do you *know*? How many reasons have you given them to reveal themselves? How do you serve them better as a result?

Discussion. After unique users and pageviews, comments are the next most flawed measure of engagement. The problem with bragging about how many comments a forum or an article draws is that too often, a few people are responsible for the vast majority of comments, flooding out the views of others and setting the tone — often uncivil to abysmal — for discussion. Look at a particularly hot thread on Huffington Post or the Guardian's Comment is Free: hundreds, even thousands of comments are impossible to read, so what does it accomplish? One could argue that hundreds of people cared enough to have their say and the news organization gave them that opportunity. But the commenters may indicate little about the larger public. And besides, in gauging the worth of both conversation and engagement, it's value we should be seeking — intelligence, reasoned debate, contributions of information and expertise — and not mere volume, in either sense of the word.

When the Guardian started its opinion site Comment is Free, it — like other news organizations — was overwhelmed with the nastiness of much of the discourse. Editors quickly learned that more resources had to be devoted to policing the trolls, killing off-topic and rude comments, banning comments around some inevitably fiery topics (namely the Middle East), and generally cleaning up the neighborhood. In the early days of commenting, I witnessed a misplaced expectation for what comment should be. Journalists expected an online publication to exhibit the same standards as their print product, where every word had worth, where facts were verified, where incivility — without at least the fig leaf of British irony — would be unacceptable. But our first mistake was to see the internet as a medium and what appears there as content. No, the net is a place, a street corner or a bar where oftentimes people are just talking amongst themselves. That has value: to hear the public speak, to understand what people are thinking, to be open, to enable connections. And so comments are worthwhile. But comments are not the end-game of engagement. Indeed, the structure of comments is essentially flawed. The form itself says that we don't want to hear from the public until after we are finished with our work, and then we will deign to allow them to say something — but by then, we've left the office and we're not listening. Comments are a lower form of interactivity and engagement. There is is a higher form:

Collaboration: Working with the public to accomplish something of worth clearly has greater value than mere blather. It also holds the community-as-collaborators in higher esteem. One common form of collaboration is crowdsourcing, which can accomplish good things but can itself be condescending, involving the public in the process of reporting already underway to accomplish goals we journalists have already decided upon, without the opportunity to hear the needs, desires, and ideas of our collaborators.

The goal — for a news organization or even a product manufacturer — should be to move the public up the production chain from purchase and consumption to design and even conceptualization. A tech company does that when it releases a product as a beta — confessing its imperfection and thus asking for users' help. Quirky.com, which makes and sells neat gadgets, not only solicits inventions from the public but relies on the public to help decide which products to make and also to improve design as well as branding and marketing. A new car company called Local Motors collaboratively designs cars, involving customers at every step using a smart system to reward the truly engaged, but also requiring the CEO to assure that the end product will be safe and economical. Collaborating in an enterprise of Google's scale or in the manufacture of physical products is more complex than joining together to comb through documents or share high-school game scores for news organizations, wouldn't you say?

Membership: News organizations, blogs, and technology companies are members of an ecosystem of information in their communities. They are also members of the communities themselves. They each have a say in the community and in being informed about it. Shouldn't members of the community have a stake in deciding how journalistic resources are being used? Shouldn't they have a voice in discussing the priorities governing the work of a news organization?

When we hear the word "membership" in the U.S. it tends to be in the context of supporting public radio or television. Membership is an appealing concept. It allows individuals to stand up and support a media entity with a not-for-profit mission — albeit one that is also still supported by underwriters (read: sponsors) who buy commercials. But what privileges of membership do these loyal viewers and listeners really get, past the tote bag?

Alan Rusbridger, editor-in-chief of the Guardian, has been fascinated with the idea of membership in news. He aspires to the model of the Barcelona football team (and Green Bay Packers), where fans are members and members are co-owners who have a voice in key team decisions. Would we in news be willing to lose some power and control over our scarce resources and ask: "Hi, I'm Sally. I'm your journalist. What should I cover today?" We've seen baby steps in that direction: a newspaper streams the news meeting over the net or lists three stories and asks which should appear on the front page. One small news site lets users change the headline over a story, to one of three editor-approved versions. Gawker Media founder Nick Denton goes the farthest, as is his habit, blurring the line between writer and reader. He allows readers to rewrite headlines and ledes on his Kinja conversation service.[17] Much of this still smacks of collaboration as exemplified by a children's science museum: "Here, kids, are the buttons you can punch that will appear to do something, but nothing harmless and nothing of lasting impact will result."

What would it mean for members of the community to be truly engaged in news? At the high end of collaboration, a news organization and its journalists could stand ready to complete the assignments conjured up by a community: "We need to know this," the community says, "and we want you to use your power as a convener to bring us together to gather this information and then to add journalistic value to that work." True, the community could organize its own task through, say, Facebook or Twitter. But the news organization can help by convening the work, by instructing people how to meet their goal, by verifying facts, by adding context and explanation, and by offering organization.

What does a member give to become a member? Membership is seen by some as just another word for subscription: Give us your money and we will give you access to see our content. It's another way to say "customer." A member might well give money to support a journalistic endeavor but a true member will likely want some voice in return. Of course, a journalist will want to make sure that she is not co-opted by her patron's funds. Journalists should also see that members can contribute value in ways other than money: giving ideas, tips, content, promotion, effort. Membership requires an exchange of value, with each side of the transaction giving something to get something.

There is one other way to look at membership, one that does not put the news organization at the egocentric middle of the Venn diagram but at the edge: The community already exists and the news organization is just another member of it, contributing value to receive value. When I spent time working with editors and executives of the Telegraph of London, they saw clearly that they served tribes — their word — of people with shared interests: conservatives, yes, and also travelers and gardeners and people interested in arts or education or history. They properly asked how they could help those pre-existing communities do what they want to do (quoth the Zuckerberg) by providing not just reporting and content but also platforms for them to share what they know or get together or buy things. Membership is not just a tollbooth. It is a two-way street.

JOURNALIST AS ORGANIZER, ADVOCATE, AND EDUCATOR

"Community organizer" sounds like a punchline to a Fox News joke about Barack Obama. But if news organizations are to serve communities, they often need to act as community organizers to marshal the forces of communities in very practical ways: listening to their needs, drawing their attention to an issue, convening them to gather together and discuss the issue, urging them to action, and helping them reach their goals. That would seem to violate our professional myths of objectivity and distance — that, like the crew of the Starship Enterprise, we operate under a Prime Directive not to interfere with other life forms, only to observe them. But the truth is that news organizations have long convened communities to take action — isn't that our desired outcome in investigative (that is, crusading) journalism: to get our readers to demand action of government, to have an impact, to bring change? I'll avoid the tired battle over journalistic objectivity and confess that on this question I have a strongly held belief: We are not objective.

If traditionalists in my field haven't already crumpled up this essay — or whatever one does in disgust, post-paper, with a digital screen — at my contentions that we are not in the content business and are not first storytellers, this may cause them to strike a match or pull the plug. Still, I'll go even farther and argue this: If it isn't advocacy, it isn't journalism. Isn't advocacy on behalf of principles and the public the true test of journalism? The choices we make about what to cover and how we cover it and what the public needs to know are acts of advocacy on the public's behalf. Don't we believe that we act in their interest?[18] As the late Columbia Journalism Professor James Carey said: "The god term of journalism — the be-all and end-all, the term without which the enterprise fails to make sense, is the public." When the Washington Post — whose former editor famously refused to vote to uphold his vision of objectivity[19] — chooses to report on government secrecy or on abuse of veterans at a government hospital or, of course, on presidential malfeasance and cover ups, that is advocacy. When an editor assigns reporters to expose a consumer scam or Wall Street fraud or misappropriation of government funds, that is advocacy. When a newspaper takes on the cause of the poor, the disadvantaged, the abused, the forgotten, or just the little guy against The Man, that is advocacy. When health reporters tell you how to avoid cancer or even lose weight, that is advocacy on your behalf. When an editor decides to cover a crime in this neighborhood but not that one, she is advocating for the allocation of attention to the first. When TV news breathlessly covers lottery jackpots with no mention of the social cost, it is advocating for a regressive redistribution of collective wealth. When a critic pans a movie to save you from wasting your money on a turkey, that is advocacy (though we don't necessarily need critics for that anymore — and I say that having been one).

What about a TV station sending a crew or a helicopter to give us video of the fire du jour, which has no wider impact than a few blocks around? Is that advocacy? No. When a TV network — not to pick on TV — devotes hours and hours to the salacious details of a crime of passion that affects none of our lives, is that advocacy? No. When an online site collects pictures of cute cats, is that advocacy? Hardly. When a newspaper devotes resources to covering football games, is that advocacy? Sorry, but no. When any alleged news organization "reports" on some celebrity's inanities, is that advocacy? No. Is any of that journalism? Under the test I put forth here, no. (And I must also confess, I worked for People magazine.)

Of course, there are limitations to advocacy. We don't want to return to the days when newspapers were the organs of political parties, doing their bidding. What separates us from that past — besides the economic support we receive from advertisers — is our independence and intellectual honesty, our ethics and standards, our credibility. That is what defines journalism versus mere advocacy. Quoting Michael Oreskes, a top editor at The New York Times and then the Associated Press: "Standards, practices, and ethics are the core. Without them, it isn't journalism." As an example of maintaining intellectual honesty, I would use the Guardian and its coverage of Edward Snowden's revelations about the National Security Agency. The Guardian's stated mission is to be the world's leading liberal voice; can't be much more of an advocate than that. Still, its NSA coverage has put a liberal U.S. administration in a most difficult bind. Thus the Guardian advocates for freedom and rights and an effective democracy, not for a political side. As a journalistic organization, the Guardian had to ask whether the public had a right to the information Snowden carried, no matter which side it benefitted (so long as the public's interests — in terms of security — were not harmed). The next issue for the Guardian was whether and how it added journalistic value. Edward Snowden, like WikiLeaks, delivered a bunch of raw and secret documents to the paper's journalists. In both cases, the Guardian added value by using its judgment to redact what could be harmful, by bringing audience to the revelations, and most important, by adding reporting to verify and explain this raw information.

So what is it then, this stuff we call journalism that doesn't advocate for people or principles, that doesn't serve a public need? At worst, it's exploitation — audience- or sales- or click- or ratings-bait. At best it's entertainment. The first is pejorative, the second need not be, for entertainment — whether a journalistic narrative or a book or a film — can inform and enlighten. But if what you do doesn't carry information that people can use to better manage their lives or their society, I'd say it fails the journalism test. Journalism-as-advocacy has been bundled with journalism-as-entertainment for economic reasons: Entertainment can draw people to a media entity and help subsidize the cost of its journalism. But it was a mistake to open the journalistic umbrella over all the content we created and called journalism. If a newspaper creates journalism, then everything its newsroom employees create in that newspaper is journalism, right? No.

So then why not embrace our advocacy and make sure it is put to good use? Why not measure the outcomes and impact of our work on the basis of what is accomplished? Why not partner with communities to use our abilities to help them meet their needs? If we do that, then we must measure our success by how much we have helped a community accomplish its goals. And we must rethink our job descriptions and the skills needed to fill them.

Alan Rusbridger, the brilliant editor-in-chief of the Guardian, talks about his idea of fast and slow journalism. Fast journalism is the obvious: covering what is happening now with updates and alerts and reports; it's what we do. Slow journalism can take many shapes. I would not define it as long-form writing; more on that later. I wonder whether slow journalism can include research of the sort universities have done, bringing greater expertise, analysis, and effort to inform the discussion of a topic and the policy developed as a result. Should a newspaper be a think tank? I wonder whether slow journalism can include advocacy: journalists and public joining together to meet common goals. The Guardian does not shy away from the idea that journalism is a cause. Should the paper and its American readers, for example, take on the end of capital punishment as a goal, bringing not only reporting but also opinion and organization to the task?

One more role for journalists to consider: educator. That does not mean we should be lecturers, continuing a one-way flow of content directed at a passive audience. A true educator empowers students to experiment, share, and build on their own, according to their abilities, desires, and needs. So, after discerning an individual's or a community's needs, journalists and their organizations can teach people how to fulfill them. As with much I've outlined here, there's not much new at the core of that notion. Service journalism has long taught readers how to accomplish what they want — to get a new job or a mortgage, to use a new technology, to understand an issue. What's new is that the net provides us with a feedback loop that allows us to see how well we succeed at advancing knowledge, understanding, and impact. Like a good teacher, we must ask whether our work leaves our users and our communities better informed, wiser, better able to meet their goals and their potential.

Earlier, I defined journalism as helping a community organize its knowledge to better organize itself. Was that too broad? Perhaps. Now I define journalism as advocacy. Is that too narrow? Yes. But in a time when journalism as a trade and an industry faces economic challenges — mortal threats, even — it is vital that we understand what we must save: the essence of journalism. Journalism is not covering fires and football and fairs. Journalism is helping citizens and communities meet their needs and accomplish their goals. Journalism is a tool to improve society. Once we have reduced journalism to an understanding of its essence — the journalism we cannot do without — then we can expand again. We need to recognize the new means that geeks have given us to meet those goals. We need to rethink the forms journalism can take to improve its effectiveness and quality. We need to cut newsrooms to their essence, find economic sustainability for that vital asset, and then start growing again. Then we can look past communities' needs to their desires. Then we can define journalism expansively. Then, yes, we can cover football and fairs. But I still want to convince TV news to stop covering every damned fire.

PART 2: FORMS

THE ARTICLE IS DEAD — LONG LIVE THE ARTICLE

I come not to bury the article but to praise it. Machined to near-perfection over a century of production, the article is ideally suited to its form. It has developed a well-defined role for each of its elements: lede imparting the latest — the news; nut graph delivering the essence of the story and telling us why we should bother to read the rest; background graph bringing us up to speed; timelines and catalogues of issues and players to set the stage; explanations to give context; quotes from various perspectives; and as many anecdotes and examples as fit in print. All this is prioritized so readers can easily navigate through and extract information and so typesetters in newspaper composing rooms with scarce time and limited space could lop off lines of type at the bottom of a story — bars of molded lead — without losing the essence of it. This is our inverted pyramid. It is the form we teach in journalism school, and with it the skills of summary and abstraction (what is the story?—perhaps the most difficult skill a journalist learns), of evidence and example, of completeness and fairness, of narrative and engagement, of prioritization and news judgment. This is the form that envelops the essential logic of journalism: that any event, issue, battle, or person can be packaged and delivered in so many lines of type. That is what we do.

Given the gifts of geeks with many new media technologies, we've enhanced the digital article, adding not just photos but slideshows, and not just slideshows but video and audio. We've added explanatory visualizations and graphics that move and interact with readers' commands. We've curated related links to give readers more from our own archives or from anywhere on the web. For good and ill, we've added comments. The article is enhanced, improved, updated.

But now let's deconstruct the article into its core assets. Let's unbundle its elements just as news publications themselves have been unbundled. Draw that inverted pyramid and its constituent elements and then imagine each as a separate entity in its optimal form. Take the background paragraph. It ill-serves everyone. If you know nothing about an ongoing story, it gives you too little history and explanation — how can you possibly hope to catch up on, say, the war in Syria in five lines of type? If you know a story well, this paragraph merely wastes your time and the paper's space; readers have had to train themselves to skip over it and find the spot where current information picks up again. The background paragraph is a compromise demanded by the one-size-fits-all constraints of news' means of production and distribution — that is, print.

Freed from those limitations, what should the background paragraph become? A link, of course: a link to an ongoing resource that is updated when necessary and not every time a related article is written. This backgrounder should be a resource a reader can explore at will to fill in knowledge. The result is more personalized, efficient, relevant, timely, and valuable for each user. The backgrounder can be created by the news organization that links to it or it can be created by anyone else and still be only a link away. It is often a Wikipedia article. The backgrounder becomes an asset, as can other parts of the old pyramid: not fishwrap that becomes worthless in a day or an hour, but something of value people return to again and again. As for other pieces of the pyramid: The explainer section of a story might be better delivered on video with a whiteboard for an expert to draw on; the timeline could be displayed as an interactive element; the list of players could include links to their bios and sites and incorporate a search for headlines about them as well as their Twitter feeds; quotes could link to the source material they were drawn from; the news, if breaking right now, might best come via Twitter rather than in the lede of a story that lags behind as it is rewritten; and so on.

A story can be made up of many assets. Once separated, the storyteller has the opportunity to present, and the reader to take, many paths through them. The well-informed reader on a topic can go straight to what's new and then leave. The novice can start with the backgrounder, then click over to an explanatory essay, then pick up on what's new. The reader need not travel to all those assets via links and clicks. The assets can come to the reader by embedding them, as Google embeds Wikipedia into its search results. Envision how the presentation software Prezi works: This PowerPoint competitor forces the creator to organize ideas into groups and then draw appropriate paths through them, paths that can be changed based on the audience. So imagine that what was an article becomes a collection of assets — the latest, the backgrounder, the timeline, the players, etc. — and that the journalist can create distinct paths among them: one for the novice, one for the expert, another for a student, another for the policymaker. Each of those assets — unlike an article in an archive — can be updated as needed. Each of the paths can be personalized based on knowledge and need.

Again, these assets need not all be created and maintained by a single source. So if Wikipedia or The New York Times has a great backgrounder, why recreate it? Link to it. Perhaps then we end up with news organizations that specialize not just in beats and topics but in kinds of assets: the latest (a wire service) or explainers (weekly publications like The Economist or Vox, a startup dedicated to the form) or relationships (a now-gone startup I worked on, Daylife, had algorithms to chart connections among newsmakers) or data (see The Texas Tribune). Of course, the people formerly known as the audience (quoth the Rosen) can also create elements of news. May the best assets win: Link to whatever best informs a user on a given path. May the best paths win: Curate the assets that best get the story across. Maybe the best editor becomes the best creator of paths. Maybe algorithms help create paths by finding the most recommended assets from the most trusted sources. In the end, articles become new molecules that bind atoms from an ecosystem of information.

What would it take to do this? Cir.ca, a mobile news application and site, takes an important step in the direction of unbundling the article. It separates elements of a news story so that the service knows what you have read — and the next time you come back, it won't repeat the same information it already gave you. It stores elements, such as quotes, separately, so they can be inserted into other stories — for example, what the president says about the German chancellor can be used in a story about him or about her, and that creates metadata around that quote, showing its relationship to various threads and people. In a Twitter discussion, Anthony De Rosa, then Reuters' social media editor and later editor of Cir.ca, said rearchitecting the article would require new culture and procedures in a newsroom.[20] Instead of thinking that we have to produce a complete article for every event and publishing cycle, we instead find or create assets and build paths, updating each as needed. When I wrote about this notion on my blog, some readers objected.[21] Jason Pontin, editor-in-chief of Technology Review, argued that articles must be self-contained. He would not force readers to follow links to get the complete story. I agree with not inconveniencing the reader. But Pontin's premise — like the presumption inherent in the form of the article — is that every reader is the same and one product can satisfy all equally. That is the core assumption mass media had to make: we shared the same interests, information, and needs. That is the fallacy and the weakness of print.

In that conversation with De Rosa, Pontin, and others, I heard journalists fret that they would need new technology — a new content management system (CMS) — to allow them to do all that I suggest. Cir.ca is built atop such a new structure. But we already have the key technology we need to disaggregate the article: the link. Case in point: A few days after the discussion, I was reading an article in The New York Times about cancers being linked to the September 11 attack on the World Trade Center. The article summarized the findings and linked to the official decision and to source material that listed every one of the 50 cancers. I am personally interested in that list, so I clicked the link. Most people would not be as interested. Their trip through the news need not be cluttered with the details I wanted. The link, in a rudimentary sense, allows The Times to give each of us different paths through the information it delivers: inverted pyramids, crafted and prioritized for each of us. Imagine how far we could take that in reinventing the form and delivery of news. The article is dead. Long live the article.

PROCESS OVER PRODUCT: ADDING VALUE TO THE FLOW OF NEWS

News is a stream of events, questions (and sometimes answers), debate, increasing information, and evolving understanding. News became a product only because it had to — to fit into publishers' and then broadcasters' space and time and production schedules. Now news can revert to nature. News never starts. It never ends. In the image of technology pioneer Dave Winer, news is a river.[22] It flows.

When Mark Zuckerberg branded his flow of updates on Facebook a "News Feed," I'll confess I was among the newsies who mocked it as a collection of mere chatter, not news. By the time Twitter came along, I knew better. Yet at first even Twitter's founders didn't realize its potential as a medium for news. As initially conceived, Twitter was meant to deliver just one constantly replaced status line per user, answering the question, "What are you doing?" According to cofounder Ev Williams, the updates were going to be private by default. Thus, Twitter never would have become a stream for news. Its fate was not self-evident.

Like a true platform, Twitter's prospects were discovered not by its creators but by its users. Those users weren't trying to be journalists broadcasting news to the world. They used Twitter simply to share what was happening around them with people they knew.

Sometimes, what is happening around you is news. "And that's why we changed the question from 'What are you doing?' to 'What's happening?'" Evans recalled in an interview. "We really liked the idea of reporters. I call them information collecting nodes — millions of them all around the world — that are reporting back about what's happening around them." When people enduring earthquakes in China or tsunamis in Japan went to Twitter to share what was happening to them, they were mostly trying to inform family and friends. But they did so in public, and so they informed the world. When Janis Krums tweeted a photo of Sully Sullenberger's plane in the Hudson River,[23] he wasn't a journalist and didn't have a media megaphone; he merely shared this astounding sight and his audience spread it far and wide and made it news. In the Arab Spring, the revolutionaries in Tunisia and Egypt — and the would-be revolutionaries of Iran before them — did not use Facebook, Twitter, and YouTube to make media. Their ambition was not to become CNN iReporters. They used these tools to find each other and to organize and act together, coordinating activities or warning of government thugs around a next corner. Embedded inside their communication was news, news that reporters, photographers, and TV cameras were not always there to witness.

Andy Carvin recognized the value of the news carried in that flow. Carvin, the former social strategist for National Public Radio, was an early virtuoso of Twitter. If he was at a conference, no one else there would need to take notes because he captured every cogent quote. Carvin had spent time in Tunisia and Egypt and knew people there. So when protests started in each country, he had the ability to call on his acquaintances and ask whether other people he saw on Twitter were really there. Were their reports accurate? Therein lies what I think will be a key skill of journalists in the future: the discernment of nodes and networks. In the past, journalists had Rolodexes of experts they could call to quote. Now those experts, as well as participants in and witnesses to news, can and do share what they know, without the need for media's intervention. A news organization will want to find and listen to those people and confirm their authority. Carvin could do that. His original contact was the node; the people around that contact were networks.

In the future, journalists must ask: How do we encourage and support flows of information? How do we add value to them? Carvin added value in many ways: He confirmed facts. He debunked rumors. He added context and explanation. He would note a witness' perspective and possible bias. He supplied background. He asked people to help him translate a video or confirm that a location in a picture was accurate. He discovered stories worthy of coverage and fed them to the NPR newsroom, which couldn't handle all his incoming tips, they told me. He became a conduit for people with news. Carvin developed tricks to find news and witnesses. For example, he'd search for phrases like "Holy shit!" and "WTF" in tweets that were shared before a news event was reported on TV or wire services. It's a good bet that those people were witnesses, not just commenters. Then he contacted those people to find out more and reach more witnesses. Nodes and networks. Most of these skills are not really new to journalists. But these skills are exercised in new ways when dealing with a story as a present-tense flow of unstructured and unconfirmed but potentially valuable information.

The Guardian prides itself on another form of news-as-flow: its live-blogging of news events. In a sense, this is a precursor to Twitter. I used to live-blog conferences I'd attend — until Carvin and his like came along and did it better on Twitter. At CUNY, we teach live-blogging because it entails different skills from writing articles after the fact. Live-bloggers must listen for the important facts and quotes flying past, capturing and sharing them while paying little heed to narrative and structure. At the South by Southwest conference in 2011, the Guardian's then-deputy editor, Ian Katz, said that devoting a writer to live-blog an event — for example, the 2012 hearings about the hacking scandal at News Corp. or a championship sports match or the London riots of 2011 — takes a considerable investment. True, I replied, but doesn't writing an article as well? Each form is used appropriately to report news. Sometimes, a Twitter stream is sufficient. Sometimes, a live blog with its freedom to write at length and embed media is better. Sometimes, an article that gives form, structure, background, and context to an event is what's needed. Sometimes, news is best served fresh. Sometimes, it's better when baked.

Who would have thought that Wikipedia would become a medium not just for encyclopedic knowledge of history but also for a flow of current information in a big news story? The platform and its users turn out to be brilliant at delivering snapshots of what we know now about a rapidly evolving event, such as an earthquake. As we think about flows of news and about news as assets and paths, the Wikipedia model performs one function of the article, bringing the reader up to speed. Unlike the article, Wikipedia is itself constantly brought up to speed by its users.

Of course, there is one other familiar form of news-as-flow: 24-hour cable news. Too often, though, the flow of actual news is insufficient to fill the time available, so cable news vamps with constantly looped video of the story at hand and numbingly repetitive narrative, which adds little.

If we reimagine news, when appropriate, as a flow to which journalists may add substance, then where does that take our work? It becomes necessary for news organizations to develop relationships with people in the places or fields they may cover so they can discern and connect with nodes and networks of witnesses and sources. The bigger and more richly veined a reporter's network as a journalist, the better position she is in when news breaks and she must call upon those she knows. That's no longer done in a Rolodex. It's done in social networks. This is the best reason for a journalist to be social: to connect with sources even before there is news.

Next, the journalist has to develop new listening skills to learn about news as it happens: See Carvin's WTF rule. This will include technology: the ability to spot news by analyzing flows of information and sensing the anomalies in it — e.g., a sudden increase in discussion of a prominent person's name should lead to the question: Why is this happening now? The news startup Vocativ says its "proprietary technology navigates the deep web, homing in on the part of the Internet that search engines can't reach, to discover the stories other news organizations cannot."[24] More and more often, the public is ahead of news outlets in discovering and spreading news . . . or rumors. A death rumor about a famous person is no reason to spread it, but it may be reason to investigate it.

If this flow of information is valuable, then it stands to reason that a news organization should encourage more of it, building or more often using platforms for communities to share information on their own, such as Twitter, Google Maps, Ushahidi, Facebook, and forums. Now imagine even 1 percent of the people walking through Times Square wearing some less-geeky successor to Google Glass, which will let any of them to shoot and share what they see in an instant. The other 99 percent will be carrying phones they can pull out to also capture and share news around them. News organizations' first reflex used to be sending a photographer to the scene, arriving after the news is over. Now its first reflex is to beg witnesses with cameras to send them their images. When a plane landed on a New York highway, drivers stopped to take and share pictures on Instagram.

Once the photos spread via Twitter, it took no time for assignment editors at TV stations and photo editors at newspapers and wire services to leave comments begging to use the images. Finding and verifying witnesses' accounts on social media is now a core journalistic skill. News Corp. bought a startup, Storyful, that makes its living discovering and verifying such accounts and media assets.

Next, imagine networks of sensors connected to the internet. Look at Safecast.[25] Established a week after the Fukushima nuclear disaster in Japan, it equipped volunteers with Geiger counters. In under a year Safecast gathered 2.5 million data points on radiation in Japan and worldwide. Safecast next raised $104,000 in crowdfounding through Kickstarter to manufacture handheld detectors that could be used by thousands more volunteers.[26] Search Kickstarter for "sensor" and you will find many more projects to manufacture sensors — or turn phones into sensors — that can be connected to the internet to report on radiation, moisture, light, noise, temperature, humidity, altitude, movement, carbon monoxide and air quality, and other environmental conditions. Consider, too, that our cars are becoming connected computers, and that appliances in our homes and offices can feed back data through the grid. What news could be found in that enormous flow of data? If traffic and noise suddenly spike or disappear at Times Square, turn to a webcam and look for tweets from people who are there to ask what's going on.

We need to work with flows of information and news both from and to the public. Now that everyone is connected everywhere, all the time, we can keep them updated constantly. I don't think we have yet perfected the art of the alert. Cable news, of course, is in a constant state of cardiac fibrillation, making anything and everything into "breaking news." When I got Google Glass, I quickly turned off both The New York Times and Twitter apps because I chafed at being interrupted for the 83rd retweet of a scrap of news or for the Times headline that would follow sometime later. Now I have an Android Wear watch and I am frustrated with alerts The Times sends every morning telling me it has 15 or 20 new stories. Well, I hope so. Jim Brady, former editor of Digital First Media and now founder of a local news startup in Philadelphia, says an alert should be worth stopping a meeting to share. An alert is an interruption. The Guardian is good at issuing alerts judiciously, for news events that are worth it. Ideally, alerts should be personally relevant. Cir.ca, the news application that unbundles news stories, allows readers to follow any particular story for updates — which, again, is made possible because Cir.ca knows what you have read and thus what would be new to you. Cir.ca can alert you about news in a story you have said you care about. Alerts should be aware of the user's context — that is, you probably care a lot more about a flood if you're driving toward it than away from it. Relevant alerts are a next frontier for experimentation in unbundled news.

CURATION

Some say "curation" is one of the most overused buzzwords of the day.[27] Guilty as charged. I use the word often because it encapsulates the value of linking in media: finding the best that already exists so you need not repeat the effort; sharing audience with work that deserves attention; complementing your work with that of others.

What does a curator do? In museums, libraries, galleries, and wine cellars, curators search for, gather, select, authenticate, add context and explanation to, present, and recommend whatever it is they collect. These are all skills needed in news today, in a new and messy ecosystem of many voices, some good and some reliable, many not. When mass media found itself competing for attention with the voices of the masses, I heard journalists again and again challenging me with the same question: How will anyone know how to find news to trust? The answer I learned to give to them and to my entrepreneurial students: Where you see a problem, find the opportunity. Engineers look for problems to solve. Journalists too often find a problem, then report on it or complain about it and stop. If there are too many voices, opinions, eyewitness accounts, and information of all sorts, then find the best. Curate.

There are a few flavors of curation: We read so you don't have to, scouring the web to find the best stuff (whether "best" means highest quality or most authoritative or most relevant); curating eyewitness accounts as Andy Carvin did in the Arab Spring (finding people who are on the scene and who are reliable); and collecting opinion or mood (here are representative, telling samples of what we used to hear on the street but now hear on Twitter). We have various means to do this: manually sifting through piles of words or images and using judgment to select what's notable; using data as signals of quality, authority, and originality (the Google way); or building platforms that allow a community to collaborate on the task of curation (voting up or down the good stuff, in the community's view, the Reddit way). In any case, the curator — to be worthy of the title — must add judgment to be more than merely an aggregator.

Sadly, too much of the aggregation and curation we've seen to date has been the product of laziness, cost-cutting, or the pursuit of easy money. It's expensive to make content, so why not just collect and link to everyone else's, rewriting it just enough along the way to get a click and serve an ad? Why not have an algorithm do what an editor used to do, losing a job and gaining cheap content? Various News Corp. executives characterize aggregation in general and Google News in particular — in descriptions aggregated by Arianna Huffington — as "parasites," "content kleptomaniacs," "vampires," "tech tapeworms in the intestines of the internet," and thieves who "steal our copyright."[28]

As early as 2009, Google Executive Chairman Eric Schmidt responded that Google News was sending one billion clicks a month — Google as a whole three billion a month — to publishers.[29] "That is 100,000 opportunities a minute to win loyal readers and generate revenue—for free," he wrote. Right. Curation — being curated — is a means of discovery and distribution for content. In an ecosystem of abundant content and no end of competitors for a reader's attention, publishers should want to be curated so that readers may find their content. Later, in a discussion of the link economy and copyright, I will explore the business implications of valuing not only the creation of content but also the creation of an audience for it — sometimes, through curation.

DATA AS NEWS

Data is (or are, if you insist[30]) the darling of the news business these days. Visualizations of data — "data viz" in the parlance — are popping up on news sites everywhere. It's so widespread that a presenter at an MIT Media Lab event in 2012 showed a slide filled with data visualizations that looked like supernovas, carnival spin art, or ripe dandelions and added the plea: "Make it stop!" Information that could be expressed in a paragraph is being stretched to fill so-called infographics that take up yards of screen space, leading to a new cottage industry in tools to create them.[31] (I fear this will do to the science of information what PowerPoint has done to the arts of narrative and discourse.) News organizations, journalism schools, and governments are busy holding hackathons to force hacks (journalists) and hackers (programmers) into arranged marriages so they can take a data set and give birth to a tool around it (everything from bus schedules for our phone to a map app built on a census of the trees that grow in Brooklyn). It's hard to have a conversation about the future of news these days without someone (often me) citing The Texas Tribune's success with data, which generates two-thirds of its traffic from users searching numbers about government salaries, prisoners, school comparisons, and much more.[32]

What we're seeing is the healthy first phase of fascination and infatuation with a shiny new tool. It's a good thing. Once journalists and users overdose on cool vizes and huge infographics and highly specialized apps, they'll be left with a new appreciation of data as a source and form of news and, I'm sure, a continued eagerness to explore new opportunities there. Data is an attitude. It is one tool that can help realize the larger ideal of openness in government, business, journalism, and society. Acquiring data and making it available to the public so anyone can investigate its meaning is an act on behalf of transparency. Before getting one's hands dirty with tables, charts, and code, journalists need to lobby on behalf of open information. News organizations should be demanding that government at every level open up and release data in standard and manipulable digital form — not paper, not PDFs — to allow anyone to share and analyze it. If they don't, we must open up government by force. I'd like to see every news organization, large and small, newspaper and blog, sponsor FOIA clubs in their communities to get scores, hundreds, thousands of citizens helping to open up data. I'd also like to see us train government in the value of sharing information so that transparency is used not just as a means to get the bastards but also as a way to work together.[33] Done right, opening data is an act of collaboration, of building platforms for shared information.

The first step in working with data, obviously, is gathering it. This means not just getting government data or other data sets that already exist. It means helping to create new data. See the section above about networks of people and sensors producing endless bits of information. See the growing if cultish quantified-self movement of people trying to measure and record everything about their lives to learn lessons from it. Tools like Ushahidi and SeeClickFix — I wish I had more examples — ask the public to gather and share their own data. A news organization collaborating with the public could pool data on local infrastructure (the proverbial pothole report) or how well-equipped schools are or how many people use parks or — here's the perennial favorite — how much gasoline costs near you. Companies alaso have no end of data that would be useful if made public: Mobile phone providers know how fast phones are traveling from cell to cell along highways; they could deliver traffic reports more accurate than anything on radio. But then Waze beat them to it. Hospitals and insurance companies know about clusters of illnesses; properly anonymized, this data could save lives. Supermarkets could compare how healthy one neighborhood's diets are versus another's. Google knows what topics interest us (and lets us compare them).[34] Where's the news in all that data? Who knows unless we can get to it.

The next step is analyzing the data. Here expertise is needed, in technology and in statistics. Some argue that every journalist should become a data jockey (and a programmer, too). I don't agree. Journalists need to collaborate with experts, knowing what's possible and being able to express their goals. They need to be technology-literate and data-eloquent. They also need competence in numeracy (a skill too many journalists pridefully lack). A bunch of numbers in a grid is pretty much useless until a viewer can dig in to identify trends, patterns, correlations, and anomalies. Sometimes, data sets will yield their secrets when joined with others — when, say, the incidence of breast cancer in an area is put atop data on pollutants and a correlation emerges. Of course, one must be cautious in reading too much into that correlation; it is not proof of cause. One must also be cautious of fetishizing data and thinking that any observation with a number at its core is worthwhile (I am reminded of Vox's observation that the Netherlands lost more citizens proportionally in the shooting down of Malaysia Airlines Flight 17 than the United States did in 9/11 — what does that signify?[35])

The next task in data journalism is presentation. This, the front-end, is the fun and flashy part. Journalists have a sense for presentation, so it's no surprise that they've taken to visualization, creating big and splashy charts, timelines, and interactive or animated graphics that try to tell a story (without necessarily writing a story). But sometimes the best presentation of data is still in text. Narrative Science uses algorithms, rather than editors, to turn structured data, such as financial reports or sports scores, into readable text articles using sets of rules (if one team scores N points over the other, then use the verb "trounce"). In a sense, text is just another form of data visualization, for we readers have been trained to garner some kinds of information more readily from a narrative than from a statistical table. A more ambitious presentation of data is an application that allows a user to explore and query the information herself, asking for facts about an address or a date or a name. That allows members of the public to ask their own questions, find their own uses and stories, and reach their own conclusions.

News organizations themselves need to be good data citizens, opening up the information they create in forms that can be shared and analyzed by others. That means giving access to archives, because once the flow of news passes into the past, it becomes data. It means adding metadata to our information — for local news organizations, there's no excuse not to have every location in a story geocoded. It means tagging stories with topics, making it possible for readers to subscribe to updates on those topics. I'd like to subscribe to notifications of corrections on stories I've read or linked to. We should also open up information about usage of our content: most popular and most emailed (which are common these days); most recommended and most commented on; and perhaps most impactful.

Data is a critical new opportunity for news organizations. What journalists have to ask — as with the flow of news — is how they add value to data by helping to gather it (with effort, clout, tools, and the ability to convene a community), analyze it (by calling upon or hiring experts who bring context and questions or by writing algorithms), and present it (contributing, most importantly, context and explanation). Witness how WikiLeaks discovered it needed news organizations — the Guardian, Der Spiegel, The New York Times — to add value to its data (which heretofore hadn't made enough of a splash) with editing and redaction, explanation, additional reporting, and — most important to WikiLeaks founder Julian Assange — distribution and publicity.

Data needs to become a mindset and a skill set in news organizations. Journalists should receive training to become literate in the opportunities and requirements of using data. Journalists also have to work with specialists who can analyze, interpret, and present data, and who can create tools allowing both reporters and the public to work with it. From a business perspective, data should be seen as an asset worth investing in, one that can yield news and new engagement often at a low cost. Data is/are a step past the article.

MOBILE=LOCAL=ME: CONTEXT OVER CONTENT

The other shiniest toy for news organizations these days is mobile, especially apps for tablets and phones. But beware a few misconceptions.

First, much of what we think of as mobile often isn't mobile at all. Most tablet usage is in the home. I often use my tablet and my smartphone when I am stationary, on the couch or at my desk or in a boring meeting. Indeed, you had better not be using these devices when truly mobile — on foot or on the road — or else you might slam into a tree. I think of mobile as a transitional term we'll use as long as we still think of smartphones as phones instead of what they really are: computers, connection machines, memory machines, assistants, toys, entertainers, maps, movie theaters, tv screens, cameras. . . .[36] Apple's Siri, Google's Glass, smartwatches, and their coming competitors may break the association of mobile with the phone when we can just speak to the air, asking questions and getting answers without having to haul out a device, without having to type or click, without going to a site or, for that matter, without ending up at a page. What happens to our notions of our products and services in news media when they are no longer built with pages at all?

As, more and more, we are able to get easy access to information and service wherever we are, through any device and via many interfaces, I think it will be foolish to organize our work around devices — a desktop product versus a mobile product — and instead we must organize it around the person: Oh, hi, Ms. Smith, we last saw you on your phone and you were asking about weather in Florida and now you are connecting to us via your laptop in Florida so now perhaps you'd like some nearby restaurants and, by the way, you'll be glad to know that the weather back home is dreary and miserable. (That pretty much describes Google Now.) Ms. Smith is mobile even if she isn't using her mobile device. Giving her relevant local information doesn't mean tying her to a postal code.

No, mobile means "around me." Mobile means context: where I am and what I'm doing. See the earlier discussion of signals — knowing who you are, where you are, where you are going, what you are buying, and so on. Mobile devices provide those signals — that context — and that is the reason Google entered the phone business, to learn more about each of us so it can serve us as individuals. Of course, this knowledge raises privacy concerns that need to be addressed by the companies gathering our signals, and certainly by government in the wake of Edward Snowden's leaks about the NSA's hoovering of data about us.[37] As I will discuss later, companies collecting data about us must give us transparency and control over data or they will lose trust and permission. But so long as value is added through this knowledge about us — and that value is delivered to us and not just to advertisers — then I believe the market will negotiate transactions using personal data to mutual benefit and with sufficient security.

Another misconception about mobile is that phone and tablet apps will recapture for media companies the control over experience, brand, and business model that the web and its links took from them. Some magazine publishers — notably Hearst — have said that selling apps has improved their post-print businesses; others have been disappointed.[38] Newspaper publishers and TV and radio stations have tripped over themselves to make apps. But I have seen private research showing that apps are frequently downloaded but rarely or never used. Bragging about the number of downloads is like bragging about how many email addresses you have, regardless of how many of your missives go unopened. I have downloaded many of the whiz-bang apps that garnered oohs with their smoothly swiped pages. They're all pretty, and we in news have much to learn from them about rethinking our idea of the page and of navigation through information. I enjoy the experience of Flipboard, Pulse, et al, and I do indeed use and like the New York Times and Guardian apps (though mostly because I can download their complete content before I get on a train that runs through a tunnel without connectivity). But I still find that I most often come to my news not through packaged experiences but instead through social links.

Apps have not proven to be news' salvation. They have many limitations. They tend to cut content off from links out to other content and links in from outside recommendations. They are expensive to make. They require marketing to get users to find, download, and use them. Though they provide a clean and controlled environment for ads, apps on the whole have not been embraced by advertisers — mostly because the audience for each app remains small. One news executive lamented to me that his mobile ads are selling for five cents per thousand views vs. $24 on his web site. It's true that when they began, apps gave designers and editors better tools to create sleek and responsive pages, but HTML5 and responsive design now make mobile web sites more appealing. On the whole, I believe making apps has proven to be a distraction for many news companies.

Am I suggesting that we ignore mobile? Hardly. Usage and traffic for mobile is fast outpacing the web. Many news sites see or are about to see a majority of their traffic from what is classified as mobile. I had a conversation with a Google executive in which I whined about functions I wanted to see added to their web services and he pshawed me, dismissing the old web as practically passé. Google is devoting itself monomaniacally to mobile, where it provides us with no end of useful and specifically built apps — mail, maps, documents, calendar, photos, entertainment, communication — that all know me as a single user. Mark Zuckerberg, meanwhile, told The New York Times that he is deconstructing his big, blue mobile Facebook application and buying or building a chain of specialized new apps — like WhatsApp, Instagram, and the beautiful Paper — to lay atop his relationships with users and his data about them.[39] Facebook's apps are built for specific uses — one for checking updates, another for instant messages and chat, another for sharing pictures, and so on. Facebook's apps all offer connections. Google's apps all offer services. Both companies' apps are built atop their relationship databases. Google and Facebook are in the relationship business. We are not.

Perhaps our problem in media is that we offer but one thing: content, or at least that is how we present what we offer. We make users come to single portals so crammed with our stuff it's hard for them to find what they want, especially in cramped mobile screens. What Google and Facebook offer instead is context in the user's terms: When you want to mail, you use the mail app; when you want to drive, you open maps; when you want to check in on friends, you open Facebook; and so on. Interestingly, both Google and Facebook have so far failed in their attempts to deliver news on web or mobile. Perhaps that was because they were trying to deliver our content without personal context.

What happens if we rethink the value of news expansively in the contexts of its many uses?

Sometimes, news is about getting alerts to the latest information. There, Twitter is decidedly beating us. I've heard TV news executives confess that they have lost ownership of breaking news (thus, when nothing is breaking, everything on TV becomes breaking news). As a platform that empowers witnesses to share and users to discover stories, Twitter is amazing. As a news product, Twitter has its weaknesses: Taken on the whole, it is disorganized; its quality depends on whom you follow and whom they retweet in turn; what you read on it is too often unreliable; it is repetitive; it overdoses. I think there is an opportunity to build services that specialize in the alert — the real alert, the kind of update that, as I said earlier, is worth the interruption, that makes the user say, "thanks for bugging me." News organizations tend to abuse the license to bother with too many headlines, too many promotions and teases carrying too little information in them. Breaking News, a Twitter account started in 1987 by Michael van Poppel, a Dutch teenager, did a remarkably good job of staying on top of big news; MSNBC.com bought the service in 2009. Since then, as we'll see next, Cir.ca has advanced the art of the breaking news alert.

Sometimes, news is about following a story. That is Cir.ca's real specialty. When you click the "follow" button on a story there, the service knows what you already know and bothers you only with what's new. One issue is that Cir.ca's small startup staff can themselves follow only so many stories, so the service cannot be personalized to every interest. With its dependence on its own staff to use its own content management system to break down the article in its unique way, Cir.ca could have trouble scaling. Or perhaps the way for Cir.ca to expand is for all news organizations to take on its structure of news and its CMS, offering updates for the stories individual readers want, only when there's something new. That would require newsrooms to radically change how they produce news — cutting it up into pieces, as Cir.ca does, to separate old bits from new bits — and how they relate to users, keeping profiles on each one to know what each wants to follow and what each has has already read. That would sound like a recipe for a reborn wire service — the update company — but when I've spoken with executives at legacy wire services about this notion, their heads explode: the utility is apparent but it is too much to imagine the work needed to change how every reporter in the field gathers and produces news.

Sometimes news is about diversion. Many presumed in the early days of mobile that everything on a phone must of course be short and quick because the screen is small and the time available brief. That is true in many contexts. That desire for nuggeted content and social sharing have given birth, for good and ill, to BuzzFeed and the listicle. But some news sites have also found that long articles can receive better readership — more time and attention — on mobile than on computers. In context, that stands to reason: stuck in a doctor's waiting room, how much better it is to dig into an article you've wanted to read than into a six-month-old issue of People (BuzzFeed beats that). So sometimes mobile is the right medium for taking in a long article. I can hear the proponents of "long-form content" hazzahing. Not so quick. I dislike "long-form content" as an organizational schema for journalism. Length is too often a criteria of editorial ego, of the hope to attract time and attention to our content. That is not the criterion that matters to the user. Quality and relevance matter. The winners in what we call long-form are services that let users collect pieces from anywhere that they don't have time to read right now, saving them for the moment when they are in that waiting room. Our challenge is making content that is so good it's worth saving and coming back to.

Sometimes news is about getting up to speed, filling in missing pieces, understanding a story that got ahead of you, getting an explanation. That is what has driven some good proportion of the usage of Wikipedia. That is what inspired the creation of Vox.com and FiveThirtyEight, new services devoted in great measure to providing explainers and backgrounders.

Sometimes news is about answering questions. When I worked as a young cub on the midnight shift at the Chicago Tribune, guys in bars would call the city desk to settle bets because libraries were closed. My editor insisted on always giving them an answer, "and preferably the wrong one," amusing himself with visions of the fights that would break out the next day when the truth emerged. Google does a great job of giving us answers to the kinds of questions we used to ask of libraries or Yellow Pages. Wikipedia does an impressive job of answering the kinds of questions we used to ask of encyclopedias. Is there a business opportunity in creating a premium service to replace the librarian and my old night city editor, or maybe employ them as human beings who can reliably answer urgent or hard questions?

Sometimes news is about recommendations — where to eat tonight, which movie to see, which phone to buy — if news media have not already ceded that function to Yelp, TripAdvisor, Foursquare, Rotten Tomatoes, Epinions, Amazon reviews, et al. Early in its web days, in 1999, The New York Times bought a service called Abuzz devoted to readers asking readers questions, such as, "Where is the best ice cream in Boston?" It folded, perhaps because it was ahead of its time or it emphasized the wrong kinds of questions or it was too limited in its scope; I don't know. I created the magazine Entertainment Weekly but if I had the same idea today — helping people decide how to spend their scarce time and money on entertainment — I wouldn't start a magazine and hire critics and make content to fill pages in print or even on the web. I'd build a platform for shared opinions among like-minded souls — thriller fans over here, romantics over there — perhaps adding a critic or two as convener and curator of the best discussions.

Sometimes news is — or should be — about connecting with others in a community of shared interest, like our neighbors. After Hurricane Irene hit the Jersey Shore, a city planner and surfer with no journalistic experience named Justin Auciello started a Facebook page called the Jersey Shore Hurricane News. It became an incredibly active hub for neighbors at the Shore — a quarter million at latest count — to share news every day. Earlier, I discussed Nextdoor as a platform to connect neighbors.

Sometimes news is about instructions — how to find a bargain or grow a garden or win at golf. There's an opportunity to rethink such so-called service content around the context of mobile devices. One of the few plausible reasons I've seen to don Google Glass is to deliver instructions while the wearer is in the midst of a task.

Sometimes news is about discussion. Sadly, much of the discussion we are subjected to — on cable networks or in website comments — is vitriolic, venal, or banal at best. Too often, it is hijacked by trolls. A 2014 study found that trolls are in fact sadists and it's nigh unto impossible to exterminate them.[40] Still, I have not given up on the art of conversation online. There have to be ways to encourage and reward productive discussion about issues that matter among sane, reasonable, smart people. In fact, our democracy depends on it.

Sometimes news now is about sharing — and sharing is about news. People share what they witness, whether that's as momentous as a plane landing in the Hudson River or as unfortunately common as a fire (alert TV news!). People share news, passing on links — often manipulated to do so by the likes of Buzzfeed and Upworthy — to inform friends or just to rack up social capital. Sharing is often misused and misinterpreted — more on that later. Nonetheless, sharing is a social trait that the internet fosters and amplifies and there are many opportunities and benefits for news organizations to help their communities share what they see, what they know, what they need to know, and what they think with each other.

Sometimes news is about taking action, helping the public or a community within it to vote, to be heard, to affect law or policy, to help others.

Whew. That is a long list of distinct uses of news: updates, follow-ups, explanation, diversion, answers, recommendations, connection, instructions, discussion, service, sharing, action. Any of those uses can be mobile. None of them has to be. Isn't that too much to expect of one site or one app? No wonder readers constantly complain of news sites: "It's so hard to find what I want." That's because we are still trying to cram a big, old newspaper into a bottomless portal on a little, tiny screen and then add all kinds of new functions and different media. We hope it will be appealing and worth the bother because it carries our brand. Perhaps we can use mobile as an excuse to rethink the value of what we offer and as a means to unbundle our services into their useful bits — as Google and Facebook do. If we allow users to declare their own needs at a particular time or in a particular place or because of a particular mood, we can better serve those needs. Perhaps mobile will force us to get better at building profiles of our users as individuals so we can serve each of them better. Mobile can make us reorganize what we offer around our users rather than around our content. Mobile isn't just another content-delivery mechanism. Don't try to be mobile first. Be user first. Context over content, that's the lesson of mobile.

REINVENTING TV NEWS

I don't want to dwell on this but I have to say that TV news — especially local TV news — sucks. It favors heat over light. It repeats much, saying little. It goes overboard on weather, sticking rulers in the snow to show how it grows or standing in the wind to prove it blows. It adores fires — which, though terrible for those in their path, usually affect few — because TV news values video über alles. It delivers **BREAKING NEWS** that isn't breaking at all but is too often long-over, repetitive, obvious, or trivial. It gullibly and dutifully flacks for PR events created just for TV. It presents complex issues with false and simplistic balance. It picks fights. It talks with only the usual suspects. It speaks in the voice of plastic people. It stages reality (the shot of the reporter nodding — called a "noddy" in the UK — is for the camera only, as is the subject's stroll down the hall to nowhere in particular — that's "B-roll"). Worst of all are the location-shot stand-ups, as when network and local reporters trudged with their satellite trucks and crews to the George Washington Bridge to talk about New Jersey Gov. Chris Christie and a scandal around closed traffic lanes there — even though there were no sources, no officials, no witnesses, and no victims to speak with; in short, there was no journalism to be done there. To TV news, all the world's a stage and its people merely props. TV news wastes precious journalistic resources without holding itself accountable for the value it delivers.

But I don't want to dwell on that. Instead, I want to examine what TV could do well.

TV can convene the public to action.

TV can summarize, sometimes too well perhaps. But delivering a quick overview of what's happening is a useful function of news.

TV can curate, bringing together divergent reports and viewpoints.

TV can explain a complex topic and doesn't have to dumb it down.

TV can demonstrate.

TV can foster collaboration, having witnesses share what they are seeing and what they know.

TV can discuss and needn't shout.

TV can give voice to countless new perspectives now that everyone has a camera on laptop or phone.

TV can humanize without cynically patronizing or manufacturing a personality.

TV on the internet can now be freed from the need to fill a clock. It can expand past video.

TV can be two-way.

TV can now create assets of lasting value instead of just talk that fills time.

When TV does those things, is it still TV? I know people who are innovating with the form online and who object to calling what they do "television" because they don't want the word's baggage. But I say they should co-opt the word, revolutionizing the concept of television instead of letting it languish in its past. It's true that there'll soon be no way to distinguish among media. What used to be a text article in a print publication now, online, has video and audio; what used to be a TV story can now carry text and photos online; both can include interactivity and discussion and more. Still,

I see value in commandeering the word television because I want innovators to take over the medium itself, pressuring its legacy owners to cast off their orthodoxies and idiocies. Those not-so-old broadcast companies, though weakened by the ceaseless growth of new competitors, still have good businesses and still attract the largest news audiences. They have had little motivation to change. Even newspapers and magazines, finally able to make video, have made the mistake of trying to ape broadcast TV. Change will have to come from outside media. Allow me to speculate on a few forms this new TV news could take:

TV with many eyes and many ears: When he canceled Piers Morgan's prime-time show, CNN President Jeff Zucker said there just weren't enough people — enough "big gets" — left to interview.[41] How sadly absurd. TV keeps talking with the same big gets, the few usual suspects. But now, thanks to the fact that millions of people have TV cameras — a webcam, a laptop camera, or a smartphone camera — it is possible to interview most anyone and to bring an endless diversity of new voices to TV.

Picture, if you will, Wolf Blitzer's gigantic CNN Situation Room video wall filled by Brady Bunch boxes with someone in each square. Imagine that below their faces are their latest tweets, so we can see what each has to say. Now imagine that a host — Wolf perhaps — can point to any of those people so we can hear their views. Or fire Wolf and let the audience take over, deciding who should be heard from next. The folks in the boxes could be experts from anywhere. They could be a panel of senior citizens talking about the impact of a change in Social Security law on their lives. They could be citizens questioning a government official. Any of the people watching could, in turn, see each others' tweets or comments in a chat. Indeed, if any viewer has something worthwhile to add to the conversation, he or she could be invited to turn on the cam and join in. The prototype platform for this already exists in the form of Google+ Hangouts.

I've long wanted to make that show. Consider the genius of Fox News founder Roger Ailes. His brilliance wasn't political and it certainly wasn't journalistic; it was economic. He realized that gabbing about the news rather than gathering it would often be more compelling and get higher ratings at a much lower cost than making packages and stories — than reporting, in other words. His scheme had just one weakness: The Fox folk need someone to gab with. I know because I used to work a block away from their studio in New York and was often called in at a moment's notice to opine — until their first choice arrived and I would be given the bum's rush. When webcams were introduced, I was talking with an old friend and former boss who was a corporate executive at News Corp., and I suggested that Fox could put a cam in the home and the office of frequent commentator Andrew Napolitano. When news in a big trial broke, they could get his face and opinions on the air, avoiding chat-free silence or middlemen like me. My friend had me talk with a network VP about the notion, but the VP dismissed it out of hand because the quality was not [hear stentorian TV voice when reading this] broadcast quality. (I am relieved I was rescued from the prospect of aiding Ailes.) But soon thereafter, Fox itself was using a small camera and a satellite phone to put Oliver North on the air from the warfront in Iraq. Soon after that, I was doing regular segments on MSNBC from my den at home, talking about what those odd new beasts called bloggers were saying. Sadly, cams were a fad. They lost their cool. That's because TV used them to be hip, not to hear new perspectives.

TV can now use the cameras the public carries with them everywhere to witness news with greater immediacy and authenticity. The trick in the future will be finding and verifying the presence of people at the scene of news so they can share what they see. Tim Pool — who made a name for himself broadcasting #OccupyWallStreet protests to the web for more than 20 hours straight via his iPhone — says he was the first journalist to use Google Glass to broadcast live TV while he was working for TV's most notable innovator, Vice. Next, I think, we'll see the audience able to direct coverage remotely, asking a witness or a correspondent to go here or there or ask this question or that. On Google+, a young woman named M. Monica, whose disability makes it difficult for her to travel, has been able to enjoy trips vicariously, using Hangouts to ask someone with a camera to point it this way or that on, say, a canoe trip.[42] I'd hope that TV news would celebrate the explosion of cameras brought on by mobile technology to break down its walls.

The (very) latest: Cable news' greatest strength — breaking news — is also its greatest weakness. After an anchor has read to us what's known, she is given nothing to do but keep repeating the same facts (or speculations) and looping the same video, trying to fool us into thinking we're up to the minute when we were up to date hours ago. Well, she could go onto other news, but cable won't do that for fear that a competitor will catch a twitchy viewer's attention. Cable's addiction to fake breaking news reached its nadir, of course, in 2014 with CNN's shameless exploitation of the loss of Malaysia Airlines Flight 370, filling air 24 hours a day for weeks with absolutely no news and with humiliating speculation about black holes. "I think that if people want to be critical of CNN for over-covering a story, that's totally fine with us," CNN's Zucker told Mashable even after the network had been ridiculed by everyone from Jon Stewart to President Obama. "Clearly, the audience has spoken and what CNN did was correct."[43] Except that CNN lost that bump in audience and its credibility along the way.

Online, breaking news doesn't have to be this way, for there is no clock to fill. A news organization can tell us what it knows and then not say another word until it knows something new. Imagine if an online news service offered us the promise of (a) summarizing what is known about a breaking story now, (b) updating only when something new is known, and (c) alerting us when that occurs and giving us the choice whether to watch the latest. Video news could steal a beat from Wikipedia. So long as the provider does not abuse the privilege by sending us constant alerts — the boy crying "breaking news!" — then we can go about our business doing other productive things until there's something new to learn. The business model of cable news — imprisoning us with the false hope of something actually happening while showing us more commercials — may not support such a high-value service. But by motivating us to make frequent visits with alerts that matter, the net could make this business model work.

Explainers and backgrounders: Recall my discussion about unbundling the article into assets and paths. Wikipedia, once again, shows the way by providing background on news stories and topics. Vox.com is making that into a business. There's also an opportunity to make a business of backgrounders in video. Video is good at explaining and demonstrating; it can take us by the hand and guide us through a complex story. One of our entrepreneurial journalism students at CUNY, Christian Fahrenbach, has done just that, using video to explain stories with complex ideas or histories for a German audience (because they are animated, his videos can be easily translated for other markets). Explainers need not go crazy with computer graphics. Sometimes, a smart person simply talking with us can be effective. One of the greatest uses of graphics on TV that I've ever seen was Tim Russert explaining election scenarios on his tiny whiteboard. The business advantage of explainers and other such enduring video assets is that their value does not disappear into the wind as soon as they are seen; they gain audience, reputation, and value over time as more and more people link to and come to watch them.

Silent (mobile video) movies: Media of all sorts are looking at mobile as just another content-delivery mechanism. TV thinks this means making shorter videos. But I wonder whether the issue with video news on mobile is not time but sound. If I need to kill a few minutes waiting for a train or want to get the latest on a story via video, I'll likely not want to haul out and connect my earphones. I won't turn on the phone's speakers (and I hope no one else on the train does). This makes me think that one appropriate model for mobile video is the silent movie: text and moving images that impart information and tell a story without having to hear.

Depth: It's often said that video for the web must be short because viewers will abandon a play after — this is a moving target — three minutes. Or a minute and a half. Or 30 seconds. Vine has taken this notion to its inevitable absurdity: six-second videos. So video, the shallowest medium, gets even shallower. In certain circumstances, this quest for brevity makes sense. But online video can also be longer, much longer than TV. I watched, riveted, Vice's 42-minute report from inside ISIS. There is no shortage of documentary filmmakers who would like your attention online since they can't get it on TV or in theaters. Interviews that would be cut to two minutes or less on the air can be played out to any length online.

Every week, I appear on *This Week in Google*, a show produced and hosted by Leo Laporte on his TWiT (This Week in Tech) network. Leo, our cohost Gina Trapani, occasional guests, and I can spend an hour, often an hour and a half, sometimes even two hours yammering on about Google and related technology news. This could — and should — never be done on the mass medium of broadcast TV. But online TWiT's stable of about two-dozen shows can find their interested, loyal, and highly targeted audiences, ranging from 50,000 to 250,000 per week. You'd think that making shows for such small audiences would hardly be worth the effort. But consider that often MSNBC's audience runs only about double TWiT's, and many cable networks have audiences so small they don't show up as blips on Nielsen's measurements.

The freedom of format allows Laporte — like the interview master, Howard Stern, on his satellite radio show — to talk with someone interesting until he has satisfied every curiosity, no matter how long it takes. Online tools also help Laporte drastically reduce his cost, using inexpensive but high-definition consumer cameras in his studio (which started as one very small room in a cottage in Petaluma, California) and using webcams on laptops for cohosts such as me to join the conversation via Skype or Hangouts. Laporte breaks more rules of broadcast TV. When he makes TV, he is simultaneously making radio as some members of the audience watch live, some watch later via streaming, and a good proportion listen to audio downloads of his shows in their cars or while jogging or at work. And Laporte tears down the wall between TV and its audience via a chatroom that is always running on his network, allowing us on-camera to talk with folks who are watching, getting their questions and ideas and often relying on them to answer questions we pose — for, as Dan Gillmor has said, our audiences know more than we do. Thus TV becomes two-way at last.

TV news has so many opportunities to reinvent itself. We are starting a series of events at CUNY and my colleagues there are teaching a course devoted to reinventing TV news. Its rebirth is about to begin.

UNTAPPED
TECHNOLOGIES

I began this essay saying that I would not predict the future, but rather suggest a few. There are so many futures I cannot yet imagine. At CUNY, we get people to imagine new opportunities by having them play a game created by Dr. Nick Diakopoulos, now a professor at the University of Maryland. He conducted research for us cataloguing new technologies that have not yet been explored deeply for news.[44] The game has small groups of players take one card with a need that news consumers share, one card with a journalistic goal, and two cards with different technologies to brainstorm new journalistic services. Just as journalists need to find opportunity in problems, so do they need to find opportunities in technologies: the geeks' gifts of the title. Every time we see something new, we should ask whether it could serve journalism. The answer, most times, will properly be no. But sometimes opportunity, need, and innovation will conspire.

Take Rap Genius. It is a platform built to allow the annotation of hip hop lyrics (and surprisingly, it did not bring cries of copyright violation from artists, many of whom were wise enough to see that Rap Genius gave them a new way to engage with their fans and explain their art). Who'd think that this platform could have application for news? Its offshoot, News Genius, has been used to annotate presidential speeches and government statistical reports and interview transcripts. Authors have put up chapters of books to supply a back story.

Medium, a new content platform created by Blogger and Twitter cofounder Ev Williams, similarly allows readers and authors to comment not at the end of articles but next to any phrase or any idea, making commenting more civil and writing more collaborative. At the same time, Reddit — an open platform that inevitably fosters the best along with the worst of online commenting — created a new Live Thread stream to allow a limited group of editors to curate the best of the web and add information to conversations around news. Who could have imagined that silly little Twitter would become a tool for gathering and disseminating news in revolutions and natural disasters? Its own creators did not. These platforms were not created for news but have application for it if we are open-minded enough to imagine the possibilities. This way, innovation lies.

I don't want to see us use technology for its own sake. I have long-since overdosed on cool. This is why I like Diakopoulos' approach of using technology to answer a need. He identifies four news consumers needs:

1. staying informed;
2. gaining personal identity (through, for example, reinforcing one's values);
3. integrating and interacting socially (finding the basis for conversation); and
4. being entertained.

He next defines 10 key journalistic functions:

1. truth
2. independence
3. impartiality
4. public interest

5. watchdogging
6. organizing forums
7. informing
8. storytelling
9. aggregating
10. sensemaking

Players in his game receive one each from those two lists and then receive cards explaining two of 27 dimensions of computing. A few examples:

- social computing (e.g., online communities and social networks);
- natural user interfaces (e.g., gesture, touch, speech);
- mobile and ubiquitous computing;
- wearable computing;
- information visualization;
- virtual reality (for example, goggles that allow the user to believe she is walking in another environment);
- augmented reality (e.g., adding information to the scene a user sees through Google Glass or a phone's camera);
- games;
- robotics;
- machine learning (that is, "algorithms that allow for the recognition of generalizable patterns or categories from data which may facilitate intelligent decisions based on such data");
- natural language processing ("algorithms that allow for the parsing and understanding of human language")
- speech recognition;
- activity recognition (for example, using sensors in a user's phone to determine where she is and how she is moving);
- data mining.

Try it yourself. Pick one news consumer need, one journalistic goal, and two random technologies. Invent, say, a social game to explain and gather solutions to a community issue. Or a network of sensors on users' phones to identify where crowds gather and to contact witnesses to whatever is happening there. Rinse and repeat.[45]

PART 3: MODELS

THE STORY SO FAR

I hear it often: News doesn't have a journalism problem. It has a business-model problem.[46] I will disagree on two counts. It is willfully blind and suicidally deaf to say that journalism doesn't have a problem when its institutions are all suffering falling audience and plummeting trust — only about a fifth of Americans have "a great deal" or "quite a lot of" confidence in news media, according to Gallup.[47] More important, to pose journalism's plight as a problem is to suggest that journalism as it *was* needs saving, that there's some fix out there that will make everything all right again if only we can find it. I prefer to state the quandary from an antipodal point of view: Journalism has no end of new opportunities and our problem is that we have not yet explored nearly enough of them.

In the first part of this essay, I explored the new relationships journalism can have with the public that it never could have before:

- understanding, interacting with, and serving people as individuals and communities rather than as a mass;
- shifting our goals, organizations, and cultures from manufacturing content to providing service, helping the public we serve meet its needs and goals;
- using, building, and offering new tools and transforming journalism into a platform with greater utility, often at scale;

- working collaboratively with the public and with fellow members of growing news ecosystems and networks;
- recasting the journalist as more than storyteller: as convener, partner, helper, educator, organizer, even advocate.

In the second part, I began to explore new forms for news that cascade from these new relationships. We can recast the article with new-media tools, then move past the article with new means of providing service: news through links, news via data, news as a flow, news through tools, news as a tool. More important than reconsidering the forms news can take is the value we can provide. Our new and richer relationships with the public we serve give us the opportunity to offer greater relevance in the context of their needs; to specialize in the journalistic skills that are most needed; to improve the quality of our work; to explore new methods to fulfill our mission. News can take on countless more forms I cannot begin to imagine because I am too old and the technologies are too new.

Now we arrive at the big question: how to sustain journalism. In this last half of the essay, I will explore business models for the new layers of news ecosystems that are supplanting the old, vertically integrated corporations that dominated news for more than a century: beat businesses, new news organizations (some of them rebuilt from the ashes of the old), networks, and platforms. For old or new news companies, I will suggest how to implement the relationship strategy as a business strategy, knowing our users better so we can increase the value we provide them and thus extend their use, engagement, and loyalty. I will suggest that knowing our users better will also yield greater value and revenue in advertising — using data about users not as a commodity to sell but as a tool to build worth. I will explore other revenue streams at small and large scale: events, digital services, ad networks, commerce, memberships, patronage, and consumer payment. I will suggest new metrics to drive our media businesses and new perspectives to consider regarding such protective concepts as copyright and intellectual property. In the end, instead of asking the question I so often hear — Who will pay for journalism? — I will ask the one that troubles me more: Who will invest in innovation? Who will help us explore journalism's many and promising but certainly unsure opportunities?

But first, we have some unpleasant business to get through. We must examine the weaknesses of the present business models for news and why they cannot carry over to our new digital world. And we need to explore further cost efficiencies, difficult as that can be. For journalism must finally reach the point at which the cutting ends so it can find ways to grow again.

DIGITAL FIRST —
WHAT THEN?

When John Paton was employed by hedge-fund investors to manage two large newspaper chains and to make sense of the combination's costs, ownership structure, and strategy, he named the enterprise Digital First Media.[48] Paton readily acknowledged that no truly modern media or technology company — no Google, Yahoo, Twitter, BuzzFeed, or Business Insider — would ever use such a phrase because they all were born digital.[49] But his newspapers — making up the second largest newspaper group in America — weren't digital. His task was to get them over what Guardian editor-in-chief Alan Rusbridger once called the big, green blob of economic uncertainty and on to the path to their digital futures.[50]

Here's how I translate the catchphrase "digital first" into a business strategy for legacy media proprietors: They must transform their companies into fully sustainable digital enterprises before the day when print becomes unsustainable. And for the most part, print will become unsustainable. I needn't explore in depth the causes of death, as the essence of mass media's plight is now apparent: Publishers as well as broadcasters controlled scarcities — limited space in print and time on the air, each in a closed distribution channel — which afforded them enviable pricing power. The net creates abundance — no shortage of content and no end of advertising availabilities, not to mention the opportunity for brands and merchants to bypass media altogether and build direct relationships with customers. That abundance drives the value of content and advertising toward zero.

Google, by contrast, has built its empire not on controlling scarcity but instead on creating and exploiting abundance. If Google had structured its business model the way legacy media companies did, it would have taken a scarcity — say, the number of people who search for "smartphones" each day — and charged what the market would bear for access to them. Instead, Google offered advertisers a better deal, charging them on performance — that is, only when a user clicked on an ad. Google built an auction to determine the market price for any search term. Google also prioritized ads on a page not on the basis of premium payment but instead on performance — the more times an ad is clicked in a given search, Google assumed, the more relevant and useful and thus productive the ad would be. Thus Google aligned its interests with those of the advertiser (and to some extent the user) and assumed the risk in the transaction — no click, no money for Google. Instead of controlling its scarcity, Google was motivated to create an abundance with its AdSense program, placing ads on any site anywhere on the net. Google analyzed the content of the site where its ads appeared, vastly improving the relevance of those ads and thus increasing the clickthrough and the revenue. And importantly, Google shared revenue with these sites, motivating them to take the ads and exploding Google's distribution at essentially no risk. The net commodified media companies' one key asset, content. Google commodified the other, distribution. Google offered media companies' advertising customers a better, safer deal, and on that foundation, Google built the behemoth that now controls more than 40 percent of digital advertising.[51]

Meanwhile, back at the ranch, publishers not only tried to protect their old-media properties, they tried to carry their old business models, assumptions, and metrics to the new, digital world. They still made content. They still sold space next to it, charging what the market would bear, which turned out to be less and less every day. When that digital advertising revenue proved insufficient to replace lost print revenue and support even a shrinking cost structure, publishers resorted to trying to charge for access to their content — and for most, that turned out not to be their salvation. Publishers tried to create and control scarcities where scarcities no longer existed. When they did try to act expansively and exploit abundance — by gathering new and larger-than-ever audiences online — they were accused of committing the "original sin" of giving away their content, their scarce commodity, for free.[52] I'll explore the arguments about paywalls below. In any case, preservation and protection turned out to be no strategy for the Google age.

The solutions for media companies may not be obvious, but the arithmetic of sustainability is: Start by reducing costs to their most essential and efficient level — assuredly a fraction of what they were for an old, vertically integrated monopoly. Then maximize digital revenue — advertising volume, yes, but I will also argue for building greater advertising value through deeper, richer relationships with consumers. Build new products and services appropriate to the new opportunities that technology presents: digital services for advertisers, mobile applications, newsletters, and so on. And explore additional revenue streams, including events, direct commerce, and consumer revenue via patronage or paywalls. Digital revenue surely will not cover the legacy costs of a deposed monopoly, but one had better see a path to digital profitability. The alternative is just to milk the old print cow until she keels over.

Print is a seductive if geriatric mistress. As I hear over and over, print still brings in the lion's share of revenue for newspaper and magazine companies. That's because advertisers and their agencies are slow to change and publishers have not been eager to educate the people who hold the checkbooks. But we must get ahead of the inevitable, which means driving the remaining advertisers to digital before they are gone. Paton started to do that by changing the bonus structure for his sales staffs — if they didn't make their digital goals, they didn't earn their print bonuses — and by getting into new advertising businesses like digital marketplaces in the belief that it is better to cannibalize thyself.

Print advertising in newspapers imploded from $65.8 billion to $17.3 billion in inflation-adjusted dollars from 2000 to 2013, with digital adding back in only $6.3 billion.[53] Classifieds are long gone. Retail continues to consolidate and in some categories collapse, a process begun well before the internet when department stores fell into each other and big-box chains replaced the local merchants that had been loyal if imprisoned customers of newspapers. Of course, the collapse of retail is only accelerating thanks to Amazon and online commerce. The result thus far: Print newspapers across America are so thin you could shave with them. The last, best economic reason to continue printing and distributing newspapers in America is to carry coupons and circulars, called free-standing inserts (FSIs) in the trade. This is precisely why you see some newspapers reducing their print frequency to the three or four days a week when they distribute FSIs. But this, too, may soon pass into oblivion. Retailers want their circulars to continue, for they can be a profit center: an opportunity to charge manufacturer brands for promotion as well as a way to sell consumers merchandise. But many of these chains are suffering because Amazon and the web have siphoned off customers, killed their pricing power, and sliced into their already-thin profit margins. Customers treat stores as showrooms and buy online. Mobile makes the situation only worse, as a potential buyer can easily comparison-shop and then order from a competitor even while standing in the store; that scenario is the raison d'être for Amazon's

Fire phone. Consumers are also getting more accustomed to using coupons on their phones rather than clipping them — giving stores or brands more data about their customers and an opportunity to target pitches and build a stronger relationship while also saving money on printing and distributing fliers. All the while, newspaper circulation keeps falling, from a high of 124 percent penetration when Americans bought multiple papers in a still-competitive market in 1950 to 37 percent penetration in 2013.[54] I asked executives at one big retail chain when newspaper distribution would drop below the point of critical mass that makes it worthwhile to continue using FSIs. They gave me a timetable that is now ticking near midnight. The real question is what will go first: the circulars or the retailers themselves.

Just to add one more kick to the kidneys for papers: Legal ads — the dense, unreadable, but highly profitable[55] public notices many governments are required to publish in publications of general circulation — are also sure to go away even over the lamentations and lobbying of newspaper publishers, as the open-data movement demands transparency of government information online. Besides, with only a third or less of Americans still reading newspapers, it is no longer possible to argue that papers are the largest distribution channel for these notices. It will soon be worth asking whether newspapers still qualify as mass media.

Magazines and television face similar pressures as newspapers, though, of course, in different circumstances. As discussed in Part 1, magazines might have squandered their opportunity to become platforms for their already-gathered communities of specific interest. General-interest magazines are suffering — what would you do if you were in charge of Time or the latest iteration of Newsweek? — while the more specialized and high-gloss magazines are being kept afloat for a while longer because they are a medium for brand advertising rather than retail or performance-based advertising. Brands and their agencies traffic in smoke, mirrors, and masses. Luxury brands particularly — inflated with marketing mystique as they are and thus cautious and slow to change — still support some magazines. But how long will that last, especially as magazines' circulation, like newspapers', is caught in a downward spiral, particularly on newsstands.[56]

On television, even as broadcast network audience shrinks like a cheap sweater and local TV news audiences follow,[57] advertising rates increase because, oddly, mass is the last scarcity in media. That is, there's nowhere else for unambitious ad agencies to get their clients' messages in front of millions of eyeballs at once — even if it is now possible with additional effort online to more precisely target advertising with greater relevance for consumers and more demonstrable return on investment for brands. It's still true that nobody ever got fired for buying Thursday night on NBC. Well, so far; upfront ad buys on TV are starting to decline.[58] Television has other artificial means of life support: mandatory retransmission fees from cable companies. Nevermind that we, the people, gave networks our broadcast spectrum in return for free and public-service programming. And nevermind that cable companies have us imprisoned with their bundles, forcing us to subsidize channels that could never make it on their own in the market. These legacy forces — brands' cognitive dissonance, ad agencies' caution, cable's monopolies, nonmarket regulation — will carry on as long their beneficiaries can squeeze another breath out of them and until new competitors like Netflix and YouTube reinvent the form and retrain the audience to be more than just an audience.

Digital will out. That reality is being exploited by no end of digital — not digital-first — competitors that can (a) start and operate at much lower cost and risk than their forebears and (b) nimbly steal away consumers and advertisers with better deals at lower cost. It's not my job here or in my university role to favor one over the other: legacy vs. startup, old vs. new. Nor is it my job to protect or fix the incumbents. It would be hubristic of me to think that I could. Still, I have my suggestions.

I will argue that publishers must set a date sooner than later when they project that print will be unsustainable or at least optional. That is, they might not dismantle their presses (unless they already, wisely, pay somebody else to do that dirty work). They could continue printing products that still bring in profit. But they must acknowledge that print will neither drive nor sustain the company past that date. And so they must push every sector of the enterprise — staff, audience, advertisers — to the digital future. As long as print survives, it should become a byproduct — not the core of the business model, not the center of the operation, not the focus of its culture. Imagine it this way: The entire staff is devoted to creating the best digital service it can. A few people in a basement room take the best of that service and repackage it, freeze-drying it for print. Print becomes a promotional vehicle for the brand's online services and a supplier of cash flow to subsidize research and development. That has been happening at some newspaper companies, including two I've worked with, Advance and Digital First, as well as some in Europe, including Axel Springer at Die Welt. The New York Times, too, is saluting the digital-first flag. Its leaked, 97-page report by a newsroom innovation committee in 2014 got the definition of digital-first almost exactly right:[59]

> Around the newsroom, this phrase often is used to refer to publishing articles on the web before putting them in print. But outside our walls, digital-first is an all-encompassing strategy.
>
> Digital-first means the top priority is producing the best possible digital report, free from the constraints of the newspaper.

The last step is repackaging the best of that digital report for the next day's paper.

This transition requires rethinking staffing, structure and work processes from top to bottom.

Companies with no legacy platform have the advantage of being able to focus entirely on creating the best digital reports. For newspaper companies, making this transition can be so challenging that several of our competitors have handed responsibility for the daily paper to small, stand-alone teams so that everyone else can focus on digital.

I might quibble with still focusing on a "report," which itself carries a number of legacy assumptions about product over service: news as content. Still, it is impressive to see the young turks behind the innovation report call upon their elders to recognize the assumptions that rule the institution. "The newsroom is unanimous," the report said. "We are focusing too much time and energy on Page One. This concern — which we heard in virtually every interview we conducted, including reporters, desk heads, and masthead editors — has long been a concern for the leadership. And yet it persists. Page One sets the daily rhythms, consumes our focus, and provides the newsroom's defining metric for success." Not just at The Times but across the industry, publications online continue to be recognizable as publications: They still make content. They still want to attract audience to that content. They still sell advertising around that content. That's less digital-first than digital-last: We will take what we know, what we have always done, and then make it as digital as we can.

Back to John Paton: I remember the day in 2012 when he charted for his advisory board — at the time, Jay Rosen, Emily Bell, and me; Clay Shirky joined later — his path to fixing Digital First's corporate structure, reducing costs to the minimum (selling every printing press, fleet of trucks, and office building that was not profitable on its own), and driving maximum revenue to digital. He explained the dynamics of working with hedge funds — a crucial factor to keep in mind when we see later how his story ends. Paton drew his projections on the whiteboard and said: OK, let's imagine that at a date only a couple of years out, we get there — the company will be substantially sustainable as a digital enterprise. Then what? he asked. What are we then?

That question inspired this essay. Trying to answer Paton's question forced me to reexamine my own thinking about the future of news, to identify and push harder against my own assumptions that sprang from my experience in legacy media: the Gutenberg context, or pressthink, as Jay Rosen would call it. Paton was asking what news *could* be, what news *should* be. What is the strategy that takes us past mere survival to reinvention? Can we get *there*? I realized that until we reimagined our destination, we would be stuck recycling the past. What's required to get to that goal is considerable imagination, experimentation, risk, failure, courage, and urgency — as well as patience.

EFFICIENCY:
THE FINAL CUT

Most discussions of the state and fate of the business of news start with revenue and a search for the means to recover what has been lost to the internet so we can pay for and thus protect newsrooms as they were. Sorry, but I will begin on the other side of the ledger with the cost of journalism. It has plummeted, not just because we have less money to spend but because we can now spend less to get and disseminate the news. Thanks to technology, specialization, and collaboration, news can be much more efficient today.

Many technologies have saved news organizations a fortune. I enjoyed reading a 1901 piece in The New York Times recounting how photographers were displacing the illustrators who used to rush to the scenes of news to sketch what they saw and who, on deadline, would describe their drawings over the newfangled telegraph to other illustrators who'd render their images.[60] A bit closer to our era, when I started in the business in the '70s, computers replaced Linotypes with digital and photographic processes to set type.[61] Next, computers allowed news organizations to "save keystrokes," in the jargon of the day, meaning that typesetters — both people and machines — were no longer needed to retype text once it had been written on a reporter's keyboard. Next, computers consolidated design and production functions, eliminating the need for large backshop operations to compose pages. All those savings, eliminating entire job descriptions, labor forces, and unions with them, came before the '80s were out. Others followed: Facsimile reproduction of pages allowed printing presses to move out of expensive city real estate into remote printing plants. Facsimile reproduction tied to satellite transmission led to the birth of USA Today and the spread of The New York Times and The Wall Street Journal as America's first national newspapers. Digital photography eliminated the need for film processing. Microfilm and then digital storage killed newspaper libraries, aptly called morgues. Technology was very good to the news industry, until it wasn't.

Even with all that disruption and downsizing, still greater efficiency and savings have been brought to news by the internet — particularly the web and its essential invention: the link, which rewards both specialization and collaboration. "Do what you do best and link to the rest" is my most quoted, retweeted, and PowerPointed utterance (it helps that it rhymes).[62] Out of that dictum flows a series of new efficiencies and necessities for news. The first is to specialize. There's little sense wasting your time writing the 25th-best account of a story when it will appear on the third page of a search request and in only a few tweets; mediocrity and repetition don't pay anymore, at least not for long. But there is considerable value in creating the best, for others will end up linking to you.

Back in the day, any metro newspaper in the U.S. had to deliver the world to its audience, who were spread just as far as trucks or trains could take the paper's early edition in a day without butting into the next city and its newspapers. (When I worked at the Chicago Tribune, our early edition, inexplicably called a "bulldog," would travel as far as Canada. Because the paper was conservative, my Republican grandmother who lived 200 miles to the south was nonetheless a loyal subscriber.) Today, of course, the world is but a click away: A reader in Chicago can get to the coverage of the Guardian, The New York Times, the BBC, or native news reports in faraway lands. So the Chicago Tribune must specialize in Chicago. It must deliver the most useful, impactful, insightful reporting on Chicago that it can. It must build a stronger relationship with the people of the region than anyone else could hope to do. If it is not the best, then the door is open to new competitors. With dwindling resources, there's no time anymore to worry about rewriting an AP story about doings in D.C. just so readers (and writers' grandmothers) will be impressed with the reportorial reach of the paper. It must do only what it can do best.

The link forces us to reexamine the scoop culture of news — the belief that being first is always worthwhile. Today the half-life of a scoop is measured in the time it takes to click. It simply doesn't pay anymore to be the first to report what will happen in a press conference when that will then be reported by hundreds of competitors, each a click away. Neither does it pay to "match" a competitor's scoop, duplicating its reporting when linking to it will do — unless your reporting does take a story further. A true scoop, something that is worth our precious resources, is an investigation that breaks new ground or an insight from a reporter who knows her beat and her community better than anyone else. The rest is just the next minute's fishwrap, digital dust.

In an age of specialization, a local newspaper — for example — will end up having to jettison most anything that doesn't serve that local mission. I don't regret the loss of local newspapers' international and national bureaus. The New Yorker's media writer, Ken Auletta, once challenged me on this point. Doesn't it make sense, he asked, for the Los Angeles Times to have an Asian bureau? Listen to that notion, I replied: one person to cover all of *Asia*? Considering the cost of such a bureau and the fact that it produces only the occasional report from a correspondent who is helicoptered in, wouldn't the paper's money be better spent and wouldn't it be a better service to international business executives and diasporal readers in Southern California to hire a few multilingual journalists in L.A. with specialties in business and politics to monitor, translate, summarize, contextualize, and link to original media from Asia? I would argue that — long before the ruination of Sam Zell's ownership — the Los Angeles Times began to lose its way and its sense of mission when it decided to shift ambition from covering its gargantuan city — which was hard enough — to opening bureaus around the country and the world in hopes of competing with The New York Times as a national power. That was its ego speaking.

As Andrew Pettegree chronicles in his painstaking history, *The Invention of News: How the World Came to Know About Itself*, the first reporters were foreign correspondents who sent their private dispatches from distant ports to their business and political patrons. The first private manuscript newsletters — made possible with the building of the first postal networks — and then the first newspapers continued to deliver foreign news in part because local news was too hot to handle with monarchs warily breathing down the necks of the earliest publishers. The invention and spread of the telegraph led to the growth of the job description of foreign correspondent, as Robert H. Patton describes in his book, *Hell Before Breakfast: America's First War Correspondents Making History and Headlines, from the Battlefields of the Civil War to the Far Reaches of the Ottoman Empire*. But those correspondents often covered events not out of relevance to the audience back home but instead for the exoticism of describing a world beyond sight and imagination. The telegraph also led to the creation of the first wire services and thus the first commodity news that many outlets could distribute at once. Yes, international and national reporting are a time-honored tradition in our business. I still hear the moans that without these bureaus newspapers will never be the same. But we mustn't limit our definition of quality to what we used to do. And where there is a vacuum, there is opportunity. I attended a meeting at Harvard's Berkman Center for Internet and Society in 2004 at which Ethan Zuckerman and Rebecca MacKinnon founded Global Voices Online, a platform that allowed so-called bridge-bloggers to read, translate, and link to bloggers reporting news all around the world.[63] Nearby, Charlie Sennott, a decommissioned foreign correspondent for the Boston Globe, founded Global Post to install reporters in cities around the world so that it could provide news to a network of publications that could, in turn, assign and thus help support these correspondents. Foreign reporting does not go away just because some newspapers can't afford to do it. If we are still lucky enough to have a few great outlets — The New York Times, The Guardian, the BBC — reporting from abroad, then we should reward them and our readers with our links to them.

Many job descriptions have already been eliminated or should be eliminated in a hard-nosed analysis of what is necessary to fulfill the targeted mission of a local publication. There's little need for the old national editor or wire editor. I will raise much dander with this statement: We can't afford copy editors any longer. Oh, I wish we could; I used to be one myself and many a copy editor saved me from many a humiliating mistake. They unquestionably assured better quality and accuracy in the work of any news organization. But if you were an editor faced with the need to cut back while still producing as much value as possible for the public, would you lay off a reporter or a copy editor? If you have the rare opportunity to hire someone new, will you hire a community engagement editor or a copy editor? The prudent editor-in-chief must think twice before retaining other luxuries once considered necessities — production editors, page designers, news editors, rewritemen,[64] movie and TV critics, business columnists, golf writers, assistant managing editors, or the expense accounts that have sent 4,000 reporters to Rome to cover the choice of a new Pope (no scoops there) or 15,000 journalists to the American political conventions (no real news there, either) — instead of keeping, or better yet adding to, the ranks of local reporters who cover and serve the community. It is unfortunate that so many people — from typesetters to arts reporters, from mailers to movie writers — have lost their jobs. But our economic reality demands harsh prioritization.

We need to reexamine whether entire sections of newspapers and magazines that were created to build audience or revenue are still worth the resources that go into them. Take — just for the sake of illustration — sports. Unless you are a paper known for sports like the New York Daily News, or you work in a sports-mad market like Alabama, odds are that your sports section attracts a minority of readers — about 20 percent in my outdated experience. When mass-media economics were in force (namely: that all readers see all ads so we charge all advertisers for all readers, a myth whose implications I will explore) then that 20 percent of incremental readership was quite valuable. But today, online, we get paid only for the ads readers actually see. And sports sections, historically, drew few ads — mostly for tires (under the sexist logic that men read sports and men buy tires). Further, there are now plenty of sites that specialize in sports — from ESPN to SB Nation, from fan blogs to the teams and leagues themselves — and most times they can do a better job of game coverage than stretched newspapers can. If pro sports coverage no longer draws audience to the rest of our reporting, if it draws fewer advertisers than other specialties, and if our coverage is inferior to what readers can find a click away, why do it? If coverage of high-school sports brings in many readers who look at that and nothing else, if there isn't advertising revenue to support it, and if the effort does not fulfill our journalistic mission, then is it better to devote reportorial resources to the topic or to build platforms that allow schools and fans to share their own scores and reports? Would those resources be better spent elsewhere, in an area of coverage in which the paper specializes?

When I've had such discussions on Twitter, I get in trouble with fans of sports coverage who point to some great writing done in its service or to investigative journalism uncovering dangers or corruption. Stipulated. But I respond by asking them what percentage of the total cost, space, and time devoted to sports qualifies as such critical journalism. How much amounts instead to game reports that could be produced by Narrative Science, the service whose algorithms take structured data like sports scores, financial results, and government information and turns them into narrative? Can we still afford to be all things to all people? We can perform similar tough-minded analyses of business, entertainment, and various lifestyle categories of coverage. Some of them certainly do bring value to readers — for example, I still want news and reviews of local restaurants, though Yelp, Foursquare, TripAdvisor, OpenTable's menus, and other platforms do a better job of giving me more information about restaurants than a lone newspaper critic ever could. It's tragic that newspapers lost out on the opportunity to build such services; if only they had thought like platform-builders instead of storytellers. Legacy news organizations need to examine everything they do and ask whether they can specialize and endeavor to be the best in each category. Then they need to ask whether the resources spent in each category will still earn sufficient revenue and audience to justify the effort. Am I suggesting that every newspaper oust its sports department? No. I am suggesting instead that every news organization perform a starkly honest audit of both the journalistic and economic value that all its activities bring under its current, unbundled business models. I use sports as a provocative example.

Just as specialization allows large enterprises to become more efficient, it also opens up opportunities for newcomers to start businesses at a small scale. Baristanet started covering just Montclair, New Jersey, then Barista Moms started serving just the mothers in town. Rather than thinking he had to start the next Wall Street Journal to cover business, journalistic entrepreneur Rafat Ali started the site PaidContent.org to cover only digital media and later Skift.com only for the travel industry. PinkNews.com covers news for gays, and before going to work for them, our entrepreneurial student Sara Sugar proposed a business to serve only lesbians — New York lesbians at that. Because you can now find your public and they you — thanks to the link — it's possible for journalistic entrepreneurs to find the sweet spot where efficiency and critical mass of audience meet at a much smaller scale than before.

Entrepreneurial journalists can now specialize not just in the subject but also in the form of news. Wikipedia happened upon its role providing backgrounders for most any topic in the news, then Vox.com saw the opportunity to create a slickly packaged commercial competitor. Cir.ca and BreakingNews.com specialize in updates and alerts. There are more business opportunities to be had in unbundling the inverted pyramid.

The other great force of efficiency brought about by the web and the emergence of news ecosystems is collaboration. Its benefits are far from fully realized. A metropolitan paper cannot afford to have reporters in every town and every town council in its circulation area — of course, it never could. But now a local news ecosystem can support many independent, hyperlocal bloggers covering suburban towns or city neighborhoods. Thus the big, old paper can link to or even embed the work of the upstarts. And the little guys can do likewise with the big paper. They complement each other, and in New Jersey we are beginning to see them collaborate with each other on reporting.

News enterprises large and small should also collaborate with the publics they serve. That volunteerism — the desire to share what neighbors know with each other, the willingness to chip in on a project of mutual benefit — is a source of nonmonetary value creation in news that is all but untapped and unmeasured, but we see the beginnings of it. In the early days of blogging, I remember many a disapproving or disbelieving editor asking how I or any journalist could have the time to devote to my site. I said that done well, blogging — and later tweeting — saved me time, for it allowed me to get help from my readers, my small but generous public. My readers give me tips and answer my questions and all too often correct me. Collaboration is not just a nice and neighborly thing to do. Collaboration is an economic necessity for the survival of journalism. But we shouldn't think of collaboration as just asking the public to do our work, crowdsourcing it. True collaborators help each other. We should help the public share and work with each other, providing platforms that allow people to connect and gather their knowledge with journalists adding value where we can. There is another layer of efficiency: The more the public can share its own information without effort and expense from us, the more information exists in a community, the less we have to do to get it, and the more we can specialize in our highest value activity: reporting. I will argue that in such an ecosystem, we can end up with more reporting than we used to have.

The news organization of the future should be specialized, expert, collaborative, efficient — and as small as it can be so it is sustainable. The bottom line: News enterprises that become profitable on their digital revenue are bound to be much smaller than their print forebears because, for all the reasons explored above, there's simply less digital revenue to be had. This hard fact forces us to redefine the core of our value and to rebuild from there rather than trying to hold onto the functions we used to perform because we've always performed them. We must cut the waste. Go to Google News, search for any current news subject of note, and see how much redundancy that exposes. On the day that I write this in 2014, I find 7,301 articles on Germany's World Cup victory, 477 on the floating of the shipwrecked Costa Concordia, 7,959 on LeBron James' return to Cleveland. As an industry, we are wasting a sinful proportion of our shrinking resources on such repetition when a link to the two or three best specialists would give users better service and save money to devote to coverage worth linking to — and to building a business based on quality, engagement, and attention rather than just volume.

What are we trying to save of journalism? I have heard many editors challenge me over the years: "How are you going to support my newsroom?" I respond that there's nothing to say their newsrooms should stay as they were. I still hear concerned citizens worry that with shrinking newsrooms, we will lose investigative reporting and watchdogs over government and powerful institutions. I worry, too. But just because we are losing jobs in large, legacy organizations — a drop of 35.5 percent from a 1989 high of 56,900 newsroom employees to 36,700 in 2013, according to the American Society of News (née Newspaper) Editors[65] — that doesn't mean that we need to lose their most important work. Here we need to continue our audit of the resources spent in what we call journalism and the return on that investment in terms of impact and value for the public. How small is the proportion of news budgets — including TV and magazines — that goes to investigations and keeping watch on the powerful? What proportion of the loss in jobs came simply through the efficiencies that resulted from new technologies? How much do we still spend today on repetition, stenography, and fluff?

This calculation leads to the obvious but critical question: What is the journalism that matters? In this essay, I have accordioned my definition of journalism as it suits the discussion at hand. I started by defining journalism quite broadly: helping a community organize its knowledge so it can better organize itself. Then I narrowed the definition of the journalism sharply to focus on the journalism that matters, arguing that if it is not advocacy, it is not journalism — that is, if it does not strive to have a positive impact on the lives of citizens, then it is not journalism. If it does not hold power to account on behalf of citizens, it is not journalism. If it merely covers the baseball game or the county fair or the latest fire, that is not necessarily journalism. Journalism changes its world. I will readily concede that is too narrow a definition of journalism. I can and shortly will expand the accordion again and argue that news should include most any means of helping communities get whatever information they need or want and, yes, that can include entertainment, sports, food, lifestyle, service, and more. But for the purposes of the harsh audit I suggest at this moment, we must use the narrow definition, identifying the journalism we must not lose or else our informed society and thus our democracy are imperiled. This is an economic calculation, a zero-base analysis of what we must protect, what we must support and sustain financially.

What is included in such high journalism? Most people begin with investigative journalism. I agree. But I don't think investigative journalism is economically imperiled for three reasons: First, it's still attention-grabbing, so news organizations old and new (see: Vice and First Look Media) will continue to do it for the gratification, engagement, awards, and branding it brings. Second, there are lots of new nonprofits — ProPublica, the Center for Investigative Reporting, The Texas Tribune, the Center for Public Integrity, to name the most prominent — now contributing to the news ecosystem with their investigations. And third, given the limited absolute dollars actually spent on investigations, it is conceivable that the investigative reporting produced now could be covered by philanthropy and patronage. But maintaining the investigative status quo is a low standard indeed; I hope that by carefully allocating resources and collaborating with others, we can increase the effort put into investigations.

Note well that investigative journalism springs mostly from two sources: whistleblowers' leaks and beat reporters' expertise. I will argue then that the most critical brick needed to rebuild the temple of high journalism is the beat. The beat reporter gains expertise in a coverage area — a town, a city hall, a cop shop, a federal agency, a field of medicine, a slice of science, an angle of the economy, an underserved community. She knows what to ask — and today, after building the new relationship with the public as I described in the first part of this essay, she can be better equipped to know what her community needs to know. She can listen for the community's questions. She knows where to find the answers — and today there are more places to look because many of the people with answers (for example, economists) have taken to blogging and speaking directly to the public. Thus it's easier to find experts or witnesses. The beat reporter gets to know the norm so she can identify the anomalies where stories lurk: For example, the lanes closed for no reason at the George Washington Bridge, a story dug up by beat reporters at The Record of Bergen County and The Wall Street Journal who weren't classified as investigative reporters but who investigated New Jersey's governor and his staff tenaciously. The beat reporter is accountable to the community she serves and — as I will explore later — can be held to account on the basis of metrics more worthwhile than pageviews and likes; she is valued on the utility she delivers and the trust she earns.

Here at last is the start of good news for the business of journalism. Once the industry has been pared to its essence and its essentials, once we determine what matters most and needs protection, once we find the means to support that work, then journalism can grow again. And I think there is a good chance it will scale not from the top down with new giants replacing the old but instead from the bottom up with beats. The reason I say that's good news: because a beat can be a business.

BEAT BUSINESSES AS BUILDING BLOCKS OF NEWS ECOSYSTEMS

In research conducted at CUNY's Tow-Knight Center in 2009 and again in 2014, modeling the news ecosystem of a market the size of Boston and then of New Jersey, we found that beats can indeed be businesses.[66] We found examples scattered across the country — and I emphasize the word scattered — of hyperlocal blogs covering towns or urban neighborhoods of about 50,000 people that were earning upwards of $250,000 to $350,000 a year, mostly in advertising revenue. It is grindingly hard work. To serve, attract, and maintain a loyal audience of sufficient size within the community, the blogger must feed the beast not merely daily but many times per day. She must constantly be out in the community, talking with people. She has to perform not just journalistic functions but also commercial functions, getting over the journalist's common phobia of business — specifically of arithmetic, advertising, and sales. To do all that alone is nigh unto impossible, so the hyperlocal blogger often works with partners — sometimes spouses — and has to earn the trust and affection of members of the community as collaborators. She also has to grapple with conflicts of interest more easily compartmentalized in large news organizations with their still-sprawling organization charts and lawyers on call — namely, how to deal with a local merchant as a reader, a subject, a source, and often an official of the town as well as a customer, while maintaining her own independence and credibility. It's tough. It's exhausting. It defeats many who try it. But still, there are many examples of success — from Baristanet to the West Seattle Blog to Red Bank Green, from The Batavian to The Lo-Down to Watershed Post.[67] These are people who care about their own communities, who want to serve them, who sacrifice their days and any prayer of vacations, who pour sweat equity into their enterprises with no hope of the exits that other entrepreneurs work toward. And thank goodness for them.

They are, as I said, a scattering. I hope to see considerable growth in these atomic units of the nascent news ecosystem. That is why at CUNY we are beginning training in beat businesses, helping journalists and others to identify communities to cover, to create their content and service, to build their advertising plans and get experience in sales, to build their marketing plans, and to get proficient at their technology platforms. In our research and modeling, we believe hyperlocal sites could increase their revenue — getting a larger share of the money that has gone to local weekly newspapers, which can exceed $1 million a year — by improving their advertising offerings, joining revenue networks, and developing ancillary revenue streams, including events and contributions. Here is what their businesses can look like:

Advertising: Most of these sites make the lion's share of their revenue selling ads to local merchants and services. Of course, these are not CPM-based (cost-per-thousand impressions) branding advertisements of the sort that large marketers and agencies buy from large media outlets. They tend to be banners and buttons and sponsorship messages — many to a page, often rotated — or enhanced directory listings for which customers are charged simple, flat fees of anywhere from $20 to $200 to $2,000 per month, depending on the size of a site's audience and the courage and negotiating ability of its proprietor.

Local blogs are innovating with ads forms. Perhaps we can blame blogs for inventing the plague now called native advertising. Bloggers invented what they called sponsored posts, which flowed in with the stream of other posts, though on responsible sites they are clearly labeled. Some sites, such as Watershed Post, are creating separate feeds of Twitter-length updates from advertisers for their home pages (real-life examples: "New Mini-Hors d'Oeuvres & Dessert Molds for All Your Summer Parties!" and "Make Perfect Whoopie Pies!"). Broadstreet Ads, an ad-serving platform based in New Jersey, invented editable ads, making it easy for merchants to change their messages often. One of my former students in Elizabeth, New Jersey, has found considerable success making videos for local restaurants and merchants, which they can use not only as ads on her site, Elizabeth InsideOut, but also on their own sites and YouTube and Facebook pages. The Tow-Knight Center is preparing a report on best practices by beat businesses in ad offerings.[68]

Digital services: Media organizations small and large need to move past selling space — no longer the scarce commodity they once controlled — to selling service, starting with the needs of the advertiser and using more tools to help them meet those needs. In this sense, media companies begin to look like advertising agencies, helping clients improve their digital lives. At Tow-Knight, we looked at the digital presences of 1,000 local merchants and services in a New York City neighborhood and a New Jersey town in 2012; what we found was opportunity: About a third of these consumer businesses and services did not have web sites and of the rest that did, only about 10 percent had been updated in a month. Almost half the businesses had no Facebook presence. About three-quarters had no

Twitter account. Even more had nothing on YouTube and yet more had no email newsletter.[69]

A local blogger or newspaper could help these businesses by building and helping to maintain feeds on Twitter, Facebook, YouTube, Instagram, Google+, Foursquare, et al — not to mention Google search. Larger newspapers have been helping clients with their SEO — search-engine optimization — for sometime. The advantage: media sites can offer fuller services with a greater share of an advertiser's spending and can gain revenue that isn't fully dependent on the site's own traffic (especially useful for a startup whose traffic hasn't yet grown to critical mass). The disadvantage: This work could be time-consuming and costly. This is why, as part of the New Jersey model, we are looking at the feasibility of shared production services for local sites.

Another issue: Many media sites don't have great digital presences themselves and there's nothing to say that agencies or new consultants couldn't beat them to the punch, offering small businesses such digital services. Media sites have a limited window of time to learn these skills and then capitalize on the trust they have with their advertising customers, offering them more services to solve more of their problems and get more revenue in the process.

Ad networks: In our recommendations for growing the business of local sites, we at Tow-Knight envisioned networks both large and small. No hyperlocal blogger can go marching into a sizable regional advertiser hoping to sell an ad that will reach a few thousand readers. But a network seller — such as the daily newspaper in a market — could aggregate the audience of all the small sites there and sell them as a package. Aren't I trying to bring mass-media economics that I've decried to these small sites? Yes, I am, because there's still money to be had in selling advertising at scale. These local sites can also sell each others' ads, so that a furniture store, say, could reach customers in five nearby towns by placing ads in five local sites for a reasonable package price.

Nascent local ad networks are emerging in some markets. Connecticut's Independent Media Network employs a salesperson to represent more than 70 independent sites and 100 local papers with an aggregate 4 million pageviews a month, splitting revenue 50/50 with network members. BroadStreet Ads in New Jersey has built functionality into its ad-serving software that allows one site to sell ads on others' sites, creating ad hoc networks to suit advertisers' needs. Of course, local sites also avail themselves of Google´AdSense and national ad networks, which tend to sell remnant advertising that can cheapen a site with irrelevant and junky ads, bringing in enough to pay for not much more than coffee. The best networks will be built on local value, giving advertisers the opportunity to reach engaged audiences for far less than monopoly local newspapers have charged. In New Jersey, we are aggregating data on the audience of the ecosystem's many sites in the hope that it can be sold to larger advertisers, allowing the network to supplement the revenue of each site in it.

Now if hyperlocal networks are such a good idea, you might ask: Why was Patch such a flame-out? Patch sounded like a good idea. Its founders saw the economics of hyperlocal: Local weekly newspapers could earn $1-3 million, starting a local blog with an inexpensive reporter — paid $25-40,000, plus a small freelance budget — and having groups of sites share sales staff to steal away even a modest proportion of what the papers earned. It seemed like a sure win. Patch had complex and secret formulas to pick the most lucrative towns to serve, starting with places that had well-to-do residents and healthy downtown commerce. But Patch didn't get its own model in shape before multiplying its mistakes across more than 900 sites. The content in Patch's sites was — pardon me — patchy. Unlike local blogs run by local people who cared about their towns, much — though not all — of Patch's content was dull, generic, and voiceless. Its audience numbers were spotty and its ad prices too high for local merchants for the performance they saw, according to advertisers I spoke with. Local sales turned out to be more difficult and expensive than Patch's founders had forecast. Toward the end of its tortured run before being sold to a private equity firm, Patch tried to compete instead with the larger daily metro newspapers, aggregating Patch sites' audiences to sell to larger advertisers. But that was no salvation.

Before they launched, I suggested to Patch's founders that they would be wise to work with the sites already in place, starting an ad network across them, sharing content to be more efficient, and concentrating on towns where there was no local blog — there are still plenty of them. This would have enabled Patch to scale across the country much faster at vastly lower cost and risk while also learning valuable lessons from local partners. But Patch refused to play well with others. I heard its executives vow to kill their small competitors. Pity. In the end, Patch was sold by Aol and denuded of staff, doing nothing to help the reputation of hyperlocal, I'm afraid.

Events: One surprise in our research of local sites' businesses — for me, at least — was how much some of them were earning through events. In Brooklyn, the Brownstoner blog started a flea market that became the core of its business and expanded into a food fair, renting stalls to vendors for $100-$220 per day. Brooklyn Based brings in sponsors and then partners with local businesses to play host to neighborhood shopping, bar, and restaurant crawls. Morristown Green runs an annual film festival and sells ads in its printed program. Other sites have held craft fairs, block parties, and other local get-togethers, which have the bonus value of marketing their services and deepening their relationships with neighbors in their communities. Brick City Live, a site in Newark run by Andaiye Taylor tried holding an event to teach local merchants how to better use the internet with the hope that she could prospect them for advertising sales. She found that the training was so valuable she could charge businesses for it, and so a new revenue stream opened up. In New Jersey, the Dodge Foundation's Local News Lab plans to run an experiment to see whether a network of sites can support a shared, itinerant event-runner to handle the time-consuming logistics of organizing events in many of their towns.

Larger sites are using events at a different scale. The Texas Tribune hired away The New Yorker's event specialist to run roundtables, debates, and festivals, earning the site $1.2 million in 2013.[70] These events have the advantage of bringing in not just a consumer clientele but also a business-to-business market (including politicians and lobbyists) and big-ticket corporate sponsors. Business-to-business sites from TechCrunch to GigaOm to Re/code to Skift, Rafat Ali's startup covering the travel industry, are holding conferences that earn both ticket and sponsorship revenue while also creating content and promotion.

Commerce: There's little money to be made in ecommerce for small or local sites now. Specialized interest-based sites can earn respectable revenue through affiliate fees by selling relevant products to their users — shoes on a shoe site, books on a book site. While Amazon has dealt death blows to local merchants with its greater efficiency and lower prices, experiments in same-day delivery by Amazon, Google, and eBay may bring some business back to Main Street. If, for example, Google or eBay allows local merchants to sell their stock to local customers online, they will need outlets to advertise. And so maybe — just maybe — there will be an opportunity for local media, large and small, to earn back revenue from retailers they had lost to the net.

Patronage: And then there's begging. Is it possible for a small site to get revenue from users? I'll discuss paywalls — charging for access to content — below. But what about voluntary contributions — patronage? In New Jersey, the Local News Lab is planning to run experiments in membership campaigns for local sites, with the aid and expertise of helpful listener-supported radio stations. We will see whether patrons will pony up to help support the work of local sites as they do for public broadcasters. Will it help to offer membership benefits: deals with local merchants; free tickets to events; matching donations from a generous patron; or, yes, T-shirts and totebags? We will find out.

We do know that some sites have run successful crowdfounding campaigns on Kickstarter or Indiegogo to launch or to pay for specific projects. Our Tow-Knight graduate Noah Rosenberg started his successful New York content site Narrative.ly by raising $54,000 on Kickstarter. The Dutch site deCorrespondent.nl raised $1.7 million on Kickstarter to launch its ambitious, subscriber-only reporting site, leading to a sequel in Germany called Krautreporter raising $1.38 million on its own. A key to these campaigns is that they give donors a choice in where to put their money and thus a greater sense of involvement and accomplishment.

Print and special reports: Because I urge news organizations to shift to their digital futures, away from their doomed print models, some think I have something against paper. I don't. Print still has its place even with beat businesses. Some of the sites we have worked with at CUNY — The Lo-Down in Manhattan, New Brunswick Today in New Jersey, and Watershed Post in New York's Catskills, plus other sites across the country — are publishing local guides and even newspapers. They find it easier to convince conservative advertisers to buy ads in print than online. Some find that print products, distributed freely in their towns or neighborhoods, are a way to promote their brands and either increase online traffic or add offline audience. Business-to-business sites similarly produce one-time or infrequent reports or white papers, delivered online and sometimes in print, as new sources of revenue.

I have concentrated here mainly on local beat businesses. But it is important to keep in mind that beat businesses, also known as single-topic news sites, can cover and serve many sorts of communities. There are a host — perhaps even a few too many — blogs and podcasts covering technology and its industry. There are blogs by economists and doctors. There are blogs covering various industries and agencies of government. The Guardian has long worked with a network of blogs covering the environment and Vox built its SB Nation business around sports blogs.

BUSINESS ECOSYSTEMS

As specialists, beats are efficient. But they are hardly sufficient to meet the complete needs of the larger community. Other, larger entities are required to complement and bring quality and scale to coverage, distribution, and advertising. These additional entities can become efficient and sustainable because together, all these enterprises, large and small, can benefit one another — if they learn to collaborate. These entities can include new news organizations, reformed legacy institutions, not-for-profit investigative organizations, public media, specialists of various sorts, networks, and enterprises I've not yet seen or imagined. Together, they make up the new news ecosystem.

In our economic modeling of this news ecosystem at CUNY, we still envisioned what we called a new news organization, also known as the "norg," a reorganized metropolitan newspaper or a successor to it.[71] The norg would find a business of scale in continuing to provide coverage of city, metro, or regional issues and news. It would be supported mostly by regional advertisers still looking to reach a large audience, in addition to new revenue streams, such as events. It could share its audience with other members of the ecosystem by curating and linking to them. Thus it would also become more efficient: probably made up of a score or two of beat reporters and editors plus technologists, where the newsroom of old was filled with hundreds of people fulfilling many job descriptions now fading from view.

In our modeling, we gave the norg another task and opportunity: network advertising sales across the ecosystem. It would aggregate the audience of the other, smaller sites and services and take that added reach to marketers that still want audiences at a metropolitan or regional scale — or national advertisers that want the opportunity to target their messages locally. This is one way that the smaller beat businesses supplement their primary revenue from the ads they sell. And it is one way that the norg supplements its own advertising revenue associated with its own content and audience, thus supporting more journalism. We've yet to see such a network emerge, but I believe it is a clear opportunity and a critical step in the development of a healthy and sustainable local news ecosystem.

Ecosystems are already supporting nonprofit, investigative news operations: ProPublica nationally; the Center for Investigative Reporting across multiple markets; The Texas Tribune and NJ Spotlight in their states; and so on. They are important contributors to the news and reporting available to the public. These operations often subsidize larger news organizations by contributing their articles to newspapers and in some cases broadcasters. Thus the investigative units get distribution and exposure — and greater impact — as well as the imprimatur of the larger organization's authority. And the larger news organization gets what amounts to free labor and free content. What's not to love?

Public media organizations — public radio and TV in the U.S. and public-service broadcasters elsewhere in the world — would do well to follow the example of these startups and collaborate as much as possible with others in their ecosystems, making finished content available to others; making raw content available for others to mine and remix; promoting and thus supporting the best work of others;

and providing technology and platforms for others' use. We are seeing examples of such efforts: WNYC in New York has been working with members of the New Jersey ecosystem on reporting projects and with members of the public on information gathering (about everything from hatching cicadas in the ground to sleep patterns of users). WNYC and the not-for-profit NJ Spotlight jointly hired a reporter to investigate post-Hurricane-Sandy recovery. WHYY and WFMU, two listener-supported radio stations, have volunteered to help us in New Jersey test membership campaigns with other sites. Public-service broadcasters in Germany are sharing content with legacy newspapers.

Whether for-profit or not-for-profit, we are also seeing the rise of what are being called single-subject news sites: something bigger than a breadbox or blog but smaller than a general-interest newsroom. Syria Deeply has gained considerable admiration for its focused, quality coverage of Syria, leading to the creation of News Deeply to make its platform available to others. Inside Climate News won a 2013 Pulitzer for national reporting. One of my favorite single-subject news sites is Chalkbeat, which covers schools — mostly in disadvantaged neighborhoods — in an odd hodgepodge of markets including New York City, Colorado, Tennessee, and Indianapolis. Its cofounder, CEO, and editor-in-chief, Elizabeth Green, has been generous in her candor with our entrepreneurial students, telling them of the pressures and conditions than can come attached to philanthropic funding. So she has worked hard to balance her funding with advertising — including for education jobs — and, to a lesser extent, events. Under her leadership and with the work of one of our graduates, Anika Anand, Chalkbeat has also been an innovator in developing new metrics of impact; more on that later. Chalkbeat raised the competitive juices of The New York Times, which started its own version, Schoolbook, which it later gave up for adoption to

WNYC. Cutbacks at the New York papers reduced education coverage, but with the start of both services, that beat may now be better served than before.

Business-to-business services also play a role in larger news ecosystems. Sites like TechCrunch and Re/code for the startup world are meant to serve readers in their industries. But they also add coverage to the larger pool of news and information and offer depth that no general-interest or even financial newspaper could provide. They give those legacy institutions somewhere to discover stories and, optimally, link to for news that would be of interest to their larger audiences. The business models are different: B-to-B sites will have smaller, more specialized audiences, which enables them to attract more focused but higher value advertising. They also run lucrative conferences, gaining revenue at the door and from sponsors. They can sell content in in-depth reports or newsletters. They sometimes offer job services and even consulting. And some of them syndicate selected content to mainstream news organizations in return for revenue or branding and promotion. It's a nice business. The more of them that exist, the more coverage of developments in business, the richer the ecosystem.

Curators and aggregators — from Google News to Huffington Post to Business Insider — also play what I say is an important role in the ecosystem. Rupert Murdoch and his loyal lieutenants have disagreed, arguing that they steal content and thus audience. In fact, these aggregators bring audience to content. They also provide an important service, scanning the ecosystem — with editors and algorithms — to find the good stuff, saving readers that laborious task and bringing attention to the best of what they find. I'll discuss the pros and cons of the link economy in greater depth below.

Of course, the people formerly known as the audience play many critical roles in the ecosystem, using various creation and social tools: WordPress, Facebook, Twitter, Instagram, Pinterest, YouTube. The public discovers, shares, and promotes news content. Given half an opportunity, the public collaborates, contributing eyewitness reports, photography and video, effort, inspiration, and more than enough opinion. The economic value of such volunteerism in the news ecosystem is criminally underestimated and underexploited. Huffington Post allows thousands of contributors to do just what the job title implies — contribute content to its site, inspiring the occasional protest that Ms. Huffington enslaves writers and devalues content. But in truth, it's the net that is the agent of content's devaluation. Huffington Post brings its audience and their attention to writers. I frequently crosspost what I write on my blog onto Huffington Post because I want the larger audience and potential influence and impact I can find there. Thus the currency I seek from Huffington Post is not dollars; it's distribution and attention. Similarly, when a reader contacts a news site with a tip, a picture of an event, or a question, she isn't necessarily seeking money — though it's still possible to sell the rare photo of the ubiquitous celebrity in tabloid-worthy pose — but may simply want to generously share information with others in the community. Or she might want others — journalists or community members — to look into a story or to offer support to a cause. Or she might just want the credit — the social capital — that comes with attention to her contribution. We must look past the unfortunate labels of "crowdsourcing" and "user-generated content," which imply that we get the public to do our work or make more stuff for us. We must realize that the public's contribution to the work of news can be valuable. The potential economic value of the public's effort is so large it seems incalculable — until some smart startup provides a platform to capture that value as, say, Twitter had done. Twitter is much more than news, of course; it's also cats. But Twitter found the way to enable and capture the value of voluntary contributions; as of this writing it's worth $22 billion. I believe there are still more and better Twitters and Instagrams and Pinterests and YouTubes to be built.

I wish I could report more success in the building of ad networks in ecosystems to facilitate the aggregation of audiences for advertisers. Some sites use remnant ad networks but those are bottom feeders, lowering the value of online advertising. Google AdSense works wonderfully for Google but in truth, most small sites I know that use it earn enough to buy the occasional latte — and they are subject to hiccups in Google's algorithms. Metropolitan newspapers have only half-heartedly tried to build such networks in their markets.

There are many roles legacy news organizations from local (a metropolitan newspaper) to international (a Guardian or New York Times or BBC) can and should play in their ecosystems besides — damnit — building ad networks. They can and should share content and audience to mutual benefit with others in the ecosystem. They should collaborate to create more journalism together than they can alone. They should promote the best work of others in the ecosystem, better serving their own readers in the process. But the greater opportunity is to rethink the very structure and work of a news organization around the existence of an ecosystem, to become a platform that enables and supports the work of others, helping communities share what they know on their own and adding journalistic and commercial value to that exchange as a supporter rather than a gatekeeper.

There's nothing to say that the legacy players — from newspapers to wire services, from photo syndicates to broadcast stations to cable channels — deserve to survive. In 2009, when we at Tow-Knight did our initial modeling of a hypothetical news ecosystem in a market the size of Boston — five million inhabitants — the Globe was threatened with sale or, failing that, folding. Though we are delighted that in the interim, the Globe has survived, innovated, and found new owners and life, we nonetheless wanted to see what its ecosystem could look like without it. A team including Nancy Wang and Jeff Mignon of RevSquare and business analyst Jennifer McFadden, led by Tow-Knight's Peter Hauck, researched and projected from known economics — revenue in advertising and other sources for successful hyperlocal bloggers; advertising rates on local sites; audience reach and frequency. They built a model with 100 small, medium, and large blogs covering towns and neighborhoods of 20,000 to 60,000 population each; plus a new news organization with a smaller but highly efficient newsroom (50 editorial employees and 90 total versus hundreds of each at the time for the Globe); plus an advertising network; and consideration for the value of the contributions of public media and volunteerism. We analyzed revenue from the bottom up — what sites of a given size were known to earn on given audience at market rates. Then we analyzed from the top down, using the Globe's own proportion of digital revenue, which at the time, like most newspapers, was running at about 10 percent of print. For that amount of proven revenue, we projected that the market could end up with an equivalent number of editorial workers to what was in the Globe newsroom at the time — almost 300 across the blogs and the new news organization. All of them would be dedicated to local coverage and would be closer to and more accountable to their communities.[72]

That vision has not been built, not yet. This is a long game and it will include — it already has included — many missteps and detours. I've already chronicled the fall of Patch. Blogs have come and gone and come still. I was particularly enthusiastic about TBD.com, a local effort in Washington run by Jim Brady. He started modeling that innovative service on a whiteboard at CUNY in a conference we held on collaborative news as he reimagined a newsroom built in an ecosystem, working with and helping support the bloggers around it.

Sadly, TBD suffered at the hands of corporate politics and was never given a chance to succeed, folding only a few months after launch. But Brady won't give up on local; as I write this, he is working on a local news startup in Philadelphia, BillyPenn.com. And in New Jersey, we are working to build the pieces of a successful, sustainable, higher quality local news ecosystem. We are getting sites large and small to collaborate and share content and thus audience — and soon, I hope, advertising revenue. We are recruiting and training beat businesses and helping them improve their advertising offerings and sales as well as site marketing. We are experimenting with events, membership campaigns, and shared backshops for advertising and marketing services. We will keep trying.

ADVERTISING, THE MYTH OF MASS MEDIA, AND THE RELATIONSHIP STRATEGY

The myth of mass media, lovely while it lasted, was this: All readers see all ads, so we charge all advertisers for all readers. The unbundling of mass media and the rise of endless competition punctures that myth and robs legacy companies of the pricing power — and monopolies — they had so enjoyed. Today, I believe we need to shift to a business built on the relationship strategy I began outlining in the first part of this essay. There, I argued that knowing people as individuals and communities — no longer as a mass — will allow us to build better services, and that, in turn, pushes us to develop new forms of news. Now I will look at how that relationship strategy can form the foundation of a stronger advertising business for news and media.

To start, if we provide our users with better relevance and value, that surely will build greater engagement, loyalty, usage, and attention, and that in turn will create more ad inventory to sell (though, granted, hardly any media company sells all the inventory it has today anyway). More important, the relationship strategy gives us the opportunity to increase the value of what we sell to advertisers.

By knowing more about who our users are, we can sell and deliver more targeted advertising that is more relevant to their customers and thus more effective. Rather than serving only one-size-fits-all "impressions" to anonymous "eyeballs" by the thousands as advertisers and media companies do now, we can offer more productive measures of value like attention, engagement, action, impact, and even sales. We can serve specific groups of users to advertisers who value them highly. With privacy properly protected, we have the opportunity to become a trusted broker of data we gather about our users. And if we get good at the relationship business, we have a brief window of opportunity to teach and sell these skills to advertisers as a service — presuming they don't wake up and learn them before we do. We also have the opportunity to move past selling advertising to selling products and services directly to users, venturing into commerce — which really is just a truncated form of marketing and advertising. The relationship strategy is one defense against the commodification of media's old content business by new competitors and new technologies.

Before exploring that chain of value enabled by the relationship strategy, allow me to return to dissect the myth of mass media, for it still has a profound impact on how we view and operate our industry. Of course, the myth was never fully true. Marketers built their own discounts into the advertising media they bought: A cosmetics brand values only the women it reaches in People magazine, not the men, so People doesn't sell all readers to all advertisers; the men are just waste. And, of course, there's the old saw from legendary retailer John Wanamaker: "Half the money I spend on advertising is wasted; the trouble is I don't know which half." Nonetheless, we can see the impact of the myth on media still. By selling all readers to advertisers, we end up valuing all readers equally and treating them all the same. This is why newspaper editors have long dreaded the day when the publisher would call and ask to cut syndication and paper costs by axing the least-read comics. The editor would commission a more-or-much-less-scientific survey to determine the laggards and then would announce the death of, say, Beetle Bailey — World War II having ended a few generations earlier. Then the editor's phone would ring, allegedly off the hook, with so many old codgers threatening to cancel their subscriptions. The paper didn't want to lose even one old subscriber, so valuable was she — just as valuable as any other. So with an abject, public apology from his executioner the editor, Beetle would inevitably be resurrected. In 2001, Star-Ledger Editor Jim Willse killed the paper's stock tables. Even after investing some of the savings in an improved business section, the paper netted $1 million to the bottom line from lower paper, ink, and syndication costs. Most others in the industry hadn't dared take this step for fear of losing subscribers. In the end, the Ledger lost only a handful of subscriptions — not even a dozen. At a dozen, that would mean that before the change, the paper had been spending $83,000 each on stock tables to hold onto those readers — some of them likely near death anyway. Earlier, I questioned the economic value of the sports section to news organizations. How many newspaper features are kept alive to retain incremental readers who may not be as valuable as other readers?

The notion of the variably valued reader represents a fundamental change in the media business model and springs naturally from a relationship strategy: We know some people better than others; we thus serve some better than others; some value our service more than others; some are more valuable to advertisers than others; some are more valuable to us than others. This should not be about rejecting less valuable readers — old Beetle Bailey, stock table, and sports fans — or redlining journalism to serve just the affluent. Instead, this equation should help us maximize the value of each relationship and let that drive our business growth. I'll explore this concept further when I discuss the idea of a reverse pay meter and the new metrics that should drive how we build value.

While busting myths, it's worth asking whether advertising itself is a myth waiting to die. You might argue that all the improvements in advertising I suggest here are mere incrementalism, adding a few dimes to the price of ads whose value is falling by dollars — and you'd be right. But to quote John Paton, when faced with earning dimes instead of dollars one has little choice but to start stacking the dimes. You might also argue that:

- media's value as a distributor of advertising is imploding under the weight of an abundance of advertising availabilities and thus plummeting prices;
- brands are themselves becoming media and producing content to both bypass and compete with publishers;
- brands are learning to build direct relationships with customers, again eliminating media as middleman;
- advertising auction marketplaces and programmatic and retargeting advertising (those ads that eerily follow you around the web trying to sell you that camera you just looked at on Amazon — more on that in a moment) are commodifying the value of both media placement and media brands;
- and Google has won the online advertising war anyway.

And you might be right again. Here's a blunter and even more obnoxious way to put the dystopic case: Advertising is failure. That is, marketing nirvana today is defined as having a great product or service that your customers sell for you. Thus the only reason to advertise is if that fails. Paradoxically, there's no better demonstration of this advertising-as-failure theorem than the rise of Google as the king of the advertising industry. Google exploded to be the most valuable brand in the world[73] not by marketing itself but by letting us users do it for them.

But here, for once, time may be on our side. Advertisers and their agencies are conservative hobgoblins of habit. Because nobody wants to argue with the guy who holds the checkbook, they are not being educated quickly. They are still buying network TV even though its audiences are shrinking rapidly — and even more surprisingly, they are paying higher rates to buy TV because they think that the mass is now becoming a scarce commodity. We will be able to sell advertising to marketers for many years to come as they continue to dragoon, brainwash, bribe, cajole, fool, beg for, and sometimes even reason with potential customers. The problem is, we in media will be able to charge them only lower and lower rates for the advertising that remains as new technologies and new competitors with new business models continue to commodify and erode the value of media.

Perhaps the ultimate blow in this commodification of media is the emergence of programmatic and retargeting advertising. Programmatic ads are bought by advertisers through artificial intelligence systems that analyze data about users — behavior, demographics — across many sites. These AI systems test ad placements and performance, automatically increasing the effectiveness of a flight of ads across the entire web.[74] Retargeting ads are the ones that follow you all around the web after you look at, say, a pair of shoes on Amazon or a hotel room on Expedia; those marketers paintball you with a cookie that lets it be known on other sites you visit that, "Here's the lady who looked at those red shoes — quick! bid to show her that ad."[75] It used to be, in both old and new media, that the advertiser had to find an appropriate, endemic environment for an ad — a fashion story for the shoes, a travel story for the hotel. Or they had to buy an ad placement based on demographics — that is, people who read Fortune can afford more expensive shoes and hotels. That's the closest they could come to making their ads more targeted and efficient. But programmatic and retargeting advertising can now deliver a specific digital ad to a given individual no matter what site she is visiting. Thus the context that media provides is worth much less than the specific knowledge that this potential customer looked at those shoes or that hotel. If Marriott knows you are interested in going to Atlanta, it doesn't care whether it serves you its ad for the Atlanta Marriott Marquis on a travel site or a business site or a sports site or a food site; ad placement on those media sites is a fungible — interchangeable — commodity. First-party data trumps mere media. This, once more, is why I am pushing a relationship strategy — so we in media can know more about our own users with our own information about them. Our relationship with individuals could end up having greater value than the content, the context, and the environment for advertising that media have long provided. We used to sell our content as premium. Now we must learn to value our relationships as premium.

If we are to improve the value of what we sell to advertisers based on more knowledgeable relationships with their customers, those relationships will be based on data. Advertisers and agencies do love data. But the data we in media have is still mostly a vestige of our mass-media business model: how many people look at our stuff how often. Tony Haile, founder of web analytics platform Chartbeat, argues that time spent with content and ads — attention, that is — is a better measure of value and is something quality media can still deliver.[76] In most cases, I think he's right. Chartbeat, which tracks users' pixel-by-pixel behavior on web pages, found in research that users have trained themselves to scroll right past the top of web pages — where sites' branding, navigation, promotion and supposedly premium banner ads reside — to get down to the meat of the matter: the content. Thus Chartbeat found that readers spend more time exposed to an ad that appears lower on a page, in the middle of a long article with which a reader is fully engaged. In internal research Chartbeat also found a correlation between time exposed to an ad and the user's recall of the ad's brand and message. This would indicate that the ads we thought were of less value, down the page, are actually of greater value than the banners we sell at a premium. Thus, Haile argues, we should be raising our prices for what we had considered secondary ads. It also tells me that news sites have been fools to cut up articles into many pieces to get more pageviews and more banner ads, which readers only scroll past — if those readers even bother with the inconvenience of clicking on the fourth or fifth page of a story that should be served on one page.

Perhaps as penance for cocreating the short attention span theater that is Twitter and the bottomless pit of content that is Blogger, Ev Williams' latest venture is Medium.com, an elegant platform meant to encourage quality writing and engaged reading of longer pieces about ideas. Medium's key metric is total time read (TTR) and Williams proposed the idea of charging advertisers by time, more like a broadcaster than a publisher. The Financial Times jumped on that bandwagon, working with Chartbeat to experiment with time-based rates.[77] Its director of digital advertising and insight, Jon Slade, told The Drum:

> We can now report back to a client and say we served you a thousand ads, and of those, 500 were seen for one second, 250 were seen for 10 seconds and 250 were seen for 30 seconds. The next obvious step is to sell blocks of time. We can sell a thousand hours of exposure to a chief executive audience in Germany, for example, or we can give clients 500 hours of exposure to finance directors in Belgium. That currency has a lot of merit.

These are new advertising models that try to move past mere ad impressions to a more valuable metric — aggregated attention — and also past an anonymous mass of users to a set of known and valued people we can deliver to marketers for more money. But we can do that only if we know them well. In the first part of this essay, I spoke about newspapers that found in-market readers were worth at least 20 times the value of out-of-market readers. I suggested that they work hard to gather not big data but small data: Do you live in my market? Where do you live? Where do you work? Speaking with other companies that, like the FT, serve business executives, I asked them to name the first data point that would help them increase both the value of their service to their users and the value of their users to advertisers. Their common answer: the industry the user works in. The next data point: the user's job title. Then followed a cascade of other still-small data points: interests (what they read), actions (whom they hired), holdings (what they own), ambitions (what job they want next), qualifications (what education and jobs they've had), and so on. Again, we in media are not built to motivate people to reveal themselves to us. That's because we are not built to give them back relevant service for that revelation. We don't have the infrastructure to collect data and maintain user profiles and then to analyze them. Media companies use behavioral data to target advertising but rarely content. They use services such as Salesforce.com to keep detailed profiles of advertising customers but not of readers. We must start with knowing people as the basis of a new business strategy, not only targeting content but creating services in response to demonstrated interest and need.

Obviously, these ideas — and the entire relationship strategy I propose — raise questions of privacy. Around the world, especially in Europe, we are witnessing a backlash — sometimes bordering on a social panic . . . or a technopanic — around fears that the internet makes it too easy for companies, governments (especially after Edward Snowden's revelations about the NSA), and nosy or ill-intentioned individuals to take our data without our knowledge and violate our privacy. I won't get into a detailed argument about the balance of privacy and publicness here; I wrote a book about that.[78] I will concede that our allied industries — media, advertising, and technology — blew it by not being open about how they were using targeting technology. That allowed The Wall Street Journal in its scare series "What They Know" to demonize the targeting cookie.[79] I've cautioned publishers from the Dow Jones to Germany's Axel Springer that by jumping on the privacy panicwagon, they may be decrying practices that are not only usually benign but that also could form the basis of a new business strategy for media companies.

The better way to approach this issue of trust is for media companies to do privacy right, to set the standard for openness: Make it clear that personal data is a currency customers can choose to use — or not — in a transaction that gives them value: greater relevance, less noise, connections with others, and (as I will suggest in the next section) discounts and other benefits. Give users transparency to their own data — what is collected and why and how it is used, and for what benefit — and the opportunity to edit that data for accuracy and comfort (making it, by the way, only more accurate and useful). Media companies can become trusted intermediaries, marketplaces, and perhaps even protectors of data.

Let's say we did these all things, that we in media become expert at building relationships. Then we also have the opportunity to take this skill to our customers, our advertisers, helping them build their digital presences and their customer relationships online. Some larger media companies do bits of that today. They help advertisers with such tasks as search-engine optimization. That's not really a core competence; truth is, media companies usually just resell the services of SEO specialists. If we in media truly knew people as individuals and understood their communities, we could help marketers break out of their bad habits of forcing messages on customers. This idea is easiest to illustrate at a small scale, say with a beat business, a hyperlocal site that serves a town. Mimicking the behavior of the local newspaper, these sites march into local merchants and sell them space on pages that advertisers then fill with their messages: "We're good electricians." But now those merchants can reach out to customers where they live online — through Facebook, Twitter, YouTube, email, Google Maps, Yelp, Instagram, and wherever customers gather next — and not just feed them messages but enter into conversations. I sat down with one family-owned business in my town and learned how the proprietor and his wife found success bringing in a new customer base — high-school students — by trading Facebook likes for discounts. The proprietor, who'd recently taken over the business from his father, also told me about the customer database he had inherited: boxes and boxes of index cards in the basement. I saw an opportunity to help him build that into a real database he could use to make targeted pitches to customers in town. I saw the opportunity to help him exploit Twitter to announce sales; YouTube to show off new styles; Google Maps to make sure his shop would be displayed well on search results there. He is far too busy to do all that. So there's the opportunity for the local beat business: It can help that merchant with his digital life. And there's a bonus. By using Facebook, Twitter, et al, the beat business can get credit for reaching more customers than its site alone can deliver, which is especially helpful as a new site grows. The disadvantage: it's all a helluva lot of work, requiring production skills and time a local site probably doesn't have. This is why, in New Jersey, we have been exploring creating shared backshops to do the work so local sites can resell their services, just as large sites resell SEO work. Thus media sites begin to look like and compete with advertising agencies, selling services and not just space.

Personal, transactional data is also key to what I believe is another revenue opportunity for media: commerce. I'm not suggesting that we open stores and warehouses, only that commerce is the ultimate and obvious extension of advertising: We help cause demand that merchants fulfill. We are compensated either via advertising or via a share of revenue; the difference is risk, whether we are paid upfront or on performance. Some media companies are beginning to sell products to the public. The New York Times is marketing not only branded merchandise — framed newspaper pages, New York Times hats, and New York Times jigsaw puzzles — but also wine and now even travel. London's Telegraph for years has sold merchandise directly to readers in categories where it would not compete with its advertisers. The Telegraph is a leading retailer of clothes hangers in the U.K., in addition to nightshirts, Panama hats, garden sheds, and — they don't much like this being known — knee braces. (I imagine the Telegraph reader is easy to spot: well-pressed, well-rested, with a jaunty hat but traces of dirt under the fingernails and a vague limp.) With one more line of direct revenue from consumers that is not available to American publishers — sports betting — commerce has added up to a considerable chunk of the Telegraph's profits. Years ago, I thought I would be fired by my newspaper employer when I dared to suggest that we should go into the real estate business, becoming a broker ourselves to acquire access to the data about homes for sale that was becoming a valuable commodity; to compete with the real-estate agents that were leaving us anyway; and to serve the customers who'd long since left for craigslist. Years later, Dean Singleton, then publisher of *The Salt Lake Tribune*, experimented with doing just that, becoming a discount listing broker. The experiment petered out in the midst of other challenges in the company, but it was a brave attempt to restructure the relationships in the market.

Next: Amazon, Google, and eBay are experimenting with same-day delivery. Years ago, I remember sitting in an industry brainstorming meeting about the future of newspapers when someone suggested that newspapers should repurpose their trucks and start delivery businesses (though given the condition of those trucks and the union status of their drivers, they probably would still be wise trying to get rid of their fleets). I wonder whether there is opportunity in retail's restructuring. Some company is going to crack local, same-day delivery, either from its warehouse (that's Amazon's model) or from local partners (that's Google's) or from any local retailer (that's eBay's). Someone will crack the far-from-trivial problem of getting local retailers' inventory computerized such that customers can find out which store has an item in stock. Pricing competition will be fierce. Margins will be even thinner than they are now. Nonetheless, someone will still have an opportunity to help create demand and benefit from it.

Could that be magazines? I was part of the team at Condé Nast that built Style.com as an online retailer. That experiment didn't succeed for a host of complex timing reasons: our fulfillment partner retrenched after the early-2000s crash; consumers weren't ready to buy expensive clothes online — though later they would be; retail wasn't our core competence; and so we were probably too soon. But if any medium would be good at sales, it should be magazines. Newspapers, too, could help drive demand, working with local partners to fulfill products as a new generation of local, retail marketing. Local media can help local merchants in other ways. On her Newark site Brick City Live, Andaiye Taylor created a loyalty program for local businesses.

NATIVE ADVERTISING: FIEND OR FOE?

Note that I have come this far in a discussion of advertising without addressing what is lately seen as the salvation of advertising and media: native advertising, sponsored content, content marketing, or whatever name it goes by this week — even <gulp!> brand journalism. That is because I think it is dangerous, the wolf in sheep's clothing. When I started Entertainment Weekly, someone plopped onto my desk the magazine industry guidelines for advertising and advertorials. A wise, old Time Inc. sage said he could summarize the entire book in one sentence: "The reader must never be confused about the source of content." But native advertising often seeks to confuse the reader, trying to trick her into clicking on what may look, sound, and smell like a headline leading to editorial content but ends up being a long and wordy marketing message. As my dean emeritus, Steve Shepard — who happened to be an author of that big book of magazine rules — complains: They refuse to use "the A-word." Advertising.

Forbes, one of the pioneers in native advertising, calls the content created by or for advertisers "brand voice" and puts a link next to that label that says, "What is this?" Well, if you have to put that link there then clearly the label isn't clear. I fear such unclear labeling could dilute the brand. In Forbes' case, the brand and company were dying when Lewis DVorkin arrived with a solution. He used the brand as candy to attract more than a thousand contributors to supplement a few score editorial staffers, reducing the average cost of content to near nil. Though I'm all in favor of publications opening up to new voices, it must be said that this tactic reduced the average quality of Forbes content. Meanwhile, on Forbes' business side, president Mike Perlis sold advertisers the opportunity to write (or have written for them) articles or posts to appear next to those written by staffers or contributors; theirs appeared under that label, "brand voice." After sometime, whenever I saw a link to Forbes on Twitter, LinkedIn, or Facebook, I came to hesitate a few beats before clicking, unsure whether on the other side of that click I'd find (1) a good piece by a Forbes journalist, (2) a good piece by a contributor, (3) a bad piece by a contributor, or (4) the wordy shilling of an advertiser. All of them lived at Forbes.com. That, to me, is the definition of a diluted media brand. The real lesson of Forbes is that there are no easy answers and quick solutions for transforming legacy media companies. DVorkin did what he could — a near miracle — with a diminished brand. He became a key tourist attraction for media executives touring New York. I know because I took many of them to meet him. He generously shared his means and methods. But I also told these executives that the path was not without peril. There are no silver bullets.

When The New York Times entered the native advertising game, it chose its words well, labeling advertisers' content as a "paid post." The Times sends more signals that this content is different by presenting it in fonts other than, well, Times New Roman — though I'm not sure what that means to readers. The company's first foray into sponsored content came from Dell. Though I was impressed with the labeling — even the URL reflects the status: paidpost.nytimes.com — I still wondered why anyone would want to read an essay from this advertiser about entrepreneurial government. What I want from

Dell is insight about technology or, more to the point, information about its computers. A later exercise for the Netflix show *Orange is the New Black*[80] received considerable praise. This article about women in prison was well-written and interesting and the feature was well-designed. But I still have to ask what this enterprise says to the reader. If this story was so compelling, why didn't the editors assign it? I have to wonder — and can never know — whether the content was softer, choosing not to tackle the roughest stuff about violence and drugs or race and sex in prison because it was meant to subtly market a comedy. I have to ask (and hate sounding haughty doing so): Is this journalism? The Times must worry whether readers will ask just that question about what they read under The Times brand. And if The Times isn't worried about confusing readers, well, that would worry me.

Perhaps I shouldn't be quite so concerned. Chartbeat has found that when readers come to a page of what I'll call, for lack of a better label, real content, they engage with it — that is scroll down through it — 71 percent of the time. But when they come to sponsored (dare I say fake?) content, they scroll only 24 percent of the time.[81] That would indicate that many see the difference. In 2014, the Interactive Advertising Bureau and Edelman, the public relations firm, conducted research with focus groups in New York and Washington and interviews with 5,000 consumers to start to define what it means to do sponsored content right.[82] Asked to distinguish sponsored from editorial content, consumers identified each correctly about 80 percent of the time in entertainment and business sites, but only half that in news sites — a troubling number. I hope to do followup research at CUNY on best practices in labeling, asking how to better assure that readers are not confused. If well-labeled, then sponsored content appearing in the flow of a web site is little different from the advertorials that filled many a page and subsidized the cost of many a journalist over the years in print. I will still wonder why, if readers ignore five words in a banner ad they are more likely to pay attention to 500 words in a paid post. But if publishers can sell it and advertisers want to buy it, if it sells products and burnishes brands and doesn't confuse readers, if done properly, should I complain?

Nobody sells native advertising better than BuzzFeed, with an entire staff devoted to creating its trademark listicles and quizzes just for sponsors: "How To Rank Your Happiness By Jars Of Nutella®" or "12 Ways Everyone Should Eat Chicken Fries, promoted by Burger King" or "13 People Who Totally Lucked Out, promoted by the New York Lottery" or "Stop Everything, IKEA Names Have Meanings." (Oops, that last one isn't sponsored content; hard to tell, eh?) Is this the secret to our salvation? In July 2014, according to Quantcast, BuzzFeed had 120 million people making almost 400 million visits.[83] In the year it was projected to earn a reported $120 million revenue.[84] It received a $50 million investment from sterling venture capital firm Andreessen Horowitz at a reported valuation of $850 million.[85] It planned to use that capital to staff up to 550 employees, a newsroom's worth of them doing decent journalism under the leadership of editor-in-chief Ben Smith. I don't buy the argument I hear that the listicles draw audience to the serious reporting; I don't see anyone breezing by BuzzFeed for "19 Cats Who Are Definitely Planning to Murder You"[86] and sticking around for the coverage of Syria. But I will buy the arguments that the journalism adds a sheen of respectability to BuzzFeed to appeal to some advertisers and that the listicles bring in the revenue to subsidize the journalism, just as journalism has always been subsidized on TV by entertainment and in newspapers by lifestyle, entertainment, fluff, and, of course, classified ads. Cats are the new classifieds.

"Ben Smith, BuzzFeed's talented editor, does not buy the argument that BuzzFeed is recreating a cross-subsidy, with frothy lists subsidizing the Russian coverage," Steve Waldman wrote in Washington Monthly. "He believes that excellent journalism is very much in their financial interest. Personally, I think he's kidding himself — and I hope he keeps on doing it."[87] Like Waldman, I doubt that listicles are journalism's salvation. I'm sure you don't want to see the The New York Times indulging in cat slideshows. Besides, as Chartbeat's research indicates, native advertising is not as effective as faddish advertisers or desperate media companies would like to believe. I'll soon cite further Chartbeat research showing that sharing isn't the indication of engagement it's been cracked up to be, either. By the time BuzzFeed's native-advertising and shared-content bubble bursts, I'll bet its founder and CEO, Jonah Peretti — the genius who also built Huffington Post into a traffic machine — will pivot to his next keen insight about media. I fear media companies will be left still trying to copy his last act.

Sponsored content is not the solution media have been dying for. Neither are listicles and quizzes. Neither are ad marketplaces. Neither were tablets. Neither, as I'll argue next, are paywalls. Media continue to grasp for straws. In one too many conference panels on this topic, I've shouted at rooms of marketers, advertising agencies, and PR people that they should not want to get into the content business. It's a crappy business looking to be rescued — hell, that's the reason I'm writing this essay. Stay away, I advise.

"So what is the answer, smartass?" I can hear you asking. I still don't know. I've suggested a few paths to explore. But that's just the beginning. We must reimagine advertising just as we rethink our core products and services and the essence of media itself: from the ground up. What does marketing look like when stores become showrooms for online marketplaces where prices and profits approach zero? I've worked with a retail executive named Shawn Samson who believes that stores and malls will become space for marketing instead of fulfillment. He's building that vision. What will marketing look like when marketers can know and even anticipate the needs and wants of customers? Yes, it's creepy to know that Target can sense when a customer is pregnant[88] but with proper and respectful transparency and control in consumers' hands, I can imagine preemptive marketing being useful — e.g., Amazon knows that when I buy a chainsaw I need oil. What could retail become when — as one of our entrepreneurial journalism graduates, Brianne Garcia, postulated in her groundbreaking business concept at CUNY — customers gain control of transactions, reaching out and asking to be sold: "Hey, fashion companies, I'd like a blouse like the one I just pinned here. Who has something nice? Who has the right price? Who wants me? I'll share the winner with my friends." What becomes of design, manufacturing, marketing, and distribution when customers become collaborators, when they move up the chain, to help select, even design, and then sell products, as they can at Quirky and Kickstarter and Local Motors? Advertising? What's that then?

In The Atlantic, Ethan Zuckerman of the MIT Media Lab declared that taking advertising was the web's original sin, leading to listicles, click bait, dark-art SEO, click fraud, and surveillance by media and technology companies. So he longed to give up on advertising and atone for the web's other alleged original sin — giving away content for free — by charging for content. I'll grapple with that suggestion next.[89] But first, I want to respectfully disagree with Zuckerman that we should give up on advertising. Apart from computerizing the purchase and serving of mass-media impressions, giving advertorials new names, and inventing the popup (for which Zuckerman confesses some unintended responsibility), we've seen precious little innovation in advertising. So even from the vantage point of a journalism school, I want to encourage and support more invention in the field. For I'm not ready to give up on advertising's support of news media.

But I will confess that my one great fear about advertising and media is that they, too, will become irrevocably unbundled, that marketers will no longer have need of media, that they will have their own direct relationships with customers without us. That is my doomsday scenario. Let's pray it doesn't happen.

PAYWALLS

If doomsday does come, who will pay for news? Someone has to, right? Who else will pay then but its consumers, yes? Isn't that the common belief?

There is no more emotion-laden topic, no fiercer battleground in the hunt for new business models for news than the discussion of paywalls. I have personally been taken to task in the once-august Columbia Journalism Review[90] and by no less than The New York Times' media critic, David Carr,[91] to name only a few, for challenging the wisdom of the wall. The arguments in favor of paywalls are apparent: Readers used to pay for content when they bought newspapers and magazines and so they should still. It was an original sin for content ever to have been given away for free online.[92] The people who use news sites the most value the content there and would be willing to pay for it, and so they should. News organizations should have multiple revenue streams so they are not so dependent on advertising alone (see: doomsday, above). And news — quality news — is expensive. Who should pay to maintain the newsroom and the Baghdad bureau? Besides, it's working at The New York Times, The Wall Street Journal, and the Financial Times, why shouldn't it work elsewhere?

My responses: I have never seen a business model built on the verb "should." Customers pay for products and services based on the value to them in a competitive market. The arguments in favor of maintaining paywalls around content tend to ignore the new reality of a media ecosystem built on abundance, no longer on a scarcity controlled by media proprietors who have long since lost their pricing power. In such a market, someone will always be able to sell a product like yours cheaper than you. Some spoiler might even figure out a way to make that product free, and it's impossible to compete with free. Nevermind that the competitor's product may not be as good. In the market, what matters in the end is this: Is it good enough? In such an ecosystem of abundance, I say it was wise, not sinful, for news organizations to open up and build an audience — bigger online than ever in print — before it could be stolen away by more efficient new competitors: from CompuServe to Yahoo, from a million bloggers to Huffington Post, from Business Insider to BuzzFeed. I will argue in a moment that if we're going to charge anyone, perhaps it should not be our most loyal, engaged, and valuable customers on whom we make money through advertising, but instead the occasional visitor and freeloader. As for the argument that news is expensive: Well, yes, it was, but we know it can be more efficient today. Besides, thanks to advertisers' support and subsidies, the truth is that readers never truly paid for news, never fully supported the cost of the newsroom. And in a competitive market, one cannot price one's offerings based on cost plus profit; that works only in a monopoly, which news organizations have now lost.

That is how the argument has gone, round and round, hotter and hotter, demonstrating little. As it has raged, newspapers have instituted paywalls by the hundreds. By this time, I think it's safe to say that the Financial Times and The Wall Street Journal should be excepted from this argument because, whether expense-accounted or not, they are bought by people who have money and need these publications and their information to make more money. The New

York Times did succeed at its second attempt to build a wall — or rather, a meter — gathering more than 800,000 paid online subscribers and changing the dynamics of the business to the point that readers now support the company more than advertisers (though, of course, advertising revenue has been falling steadily all the while). At about $200 each, the company's 800,000 digital subscribers produce a new revenue stream estimated at $160 million a year. In 2014, digital advertising revenue about equalled that amount.[93] Together, these digital revenue streams exceed the reported $220 million cost of The Times' newsroom, and that is an impressive milestone on the path to becoming a fully sustainable digital enterprise. Martin Nisenholtz, the business executive who started NYTimes.com, has told my classes that giving away Times content online was not an original sin but a foundational necessity, for The Times needed to compete with other new players and to build market share.[94] In fact, being free allowed The Times to become a truly international brand with a huge audience: almost 60 million monthly readers online vs. less than 1 million buyers daily in print.[95] Having that large an audience is what made it possible for The Times to put up its meter, for its conversion rate from online user to digital subscriber is only a bit over 1 percent, but 1 percent of almost 60 million is a lot of subscribers.

When it started to charge, The Times allowed users to see 20 stories a month for free (with various additions, including links from social media) before encountering the meter and getting hit up to pay up. But not enough people hit the wall and got the pitch. The Times lowered the barrier so customers would see only 10 stories a month for free. That means the vast majority of The Times' audience doesn't read so much as one story every three days. That is a shockingly low level of engagement for the pinnacle of a profession that considers itself vital to the maintenance of democracy and society. For lesser newspapers, the numbers are worse. According to Jeff Hartley, vice president for consumer revenue at the Morris Publishing Group, experience with Press+, the leading provider of paywall services, shows that on average 3–4 percent of users will come often enough to hit the wall and about half a percent of those stopped will pay.[96]

The Times was also well aware that by losing some audience when it turned on its meter, it faced a risk of losing advertising. By *very* rough rule of thumb, media companies these days make something like 80 percent of their revenue from 20 percent of their users — that is, their most loyal 20 percent, who come back more often and generate more pageviews and thus more ad sales opportunities. By putting a wall in the face of those loyal users, a news organization — especially one less worthy than The Times — risks losing the most valuable audience for advertisers. Two more points about the economics of The Times' meter: First, there are other costs. The Times spent millions on research and technology. There are also ongoing marketing costs for subscriber acquisition and costs for customer service. Second, the way The Times prices its offering artificially bolsters print: It's cheaper for me to subscribe to the paper and get digital "for free" than to cancel the print product we don't read anymore and pay for digital alone. Now as long as print continues to have greater advertising revenue, that makes sense, right? Yes, except one could argue that this pricing tactic only delays the inevitable, the transition to a truly digital enterprise. Witness the concern in the leaked Times innovation report about print still being central to the operation of the newsroom and the business. I wonder whether the meter could bring a hidden innovation opportunity cost by extending the life of print. Still, I give The Times considerable credit for making its pay meter a success. I value The Times and want it to succeed and continue. I happily pay my subscription every month. But just as Apple can succeed at breaking rules because it is so damned good, so The Times could succeed at not only building a paywall but also at attracting high-value branding advertisers because it is that damned good. But the Pondunk Daily Disgrace? Not so much.

According to analyst Ken Doctor, about 40 percent of America's 1,400 daily newspapers have erected paywalls. The country's largest chain, Gannett, did so and said the wall contributed $100 million in digital subscription revenue.[97] That's the good news. But after a year, its digital subscription growth rate fell to about 1 percent.[98] And its sites lost audience to free competitors. Three years after introducing its pay meter in 2011 and gathering its 800,000 digital subscribers, growth of that core digital subscription base for The New York Times — apart from new premium products — stalled at just over 1 percent.[99] John Paton infamously called paywalls "as dumb as a bag of hammers" but implemented them on his papers at Digital First, acknowledging that it was a short-term tactic to bolster cash flow. (Remember who Paton's bosses were — hedge funds — and what they expect — improved balance sheets.) I worry that other newspapers will look at themselves in the mirror and think they can do what The Times has done. But they don't have more than 50 million users every month as The Times does. Will a 1 percent conversion rate — or likely less — against a much smaller audience be worth the expense and risk of also reducing audience and thus advertising? They don't have the loyalty that The Times has. Will they have the opportunity to make a pitch that's welcomed? They don't have the higher value branding advertisers The Times has. They must depend instead on a suffering local retail industry. And let's be honest: They're just not as good as The Times, not worth the price. That is why I have taken the slings and arrows of my detractors and continued to question the business efficacy of building walls and limiting growth.

An industry facing woeful numbers in engagement and loyalty is ill-advised to be putting up barriers to audience, especially to those fewer and fewer surviving loyal users and more especially to a younger audience that has never read a newspaper. We should be finding ways to attract more people to us with better service. We should be finding new ways to go serve users where they are rather than making them come to us and then charging them once they arrive. We should be building rich relationships with the people we serve and building our businesses atop that.

Can we earn money from the people we serve? I believe we can — but not necessarily just by charging them for access to content.

PATRONAGE

So far, we have examined direct revenue from users as a matter of access and ownership: a copyright-era model. And we have dealt in one currency: money. There are other models that exchange value with users in currencies including but not limited to cash. Consider for illustration's sake the idea of a reverse pay meter, which values not just content but also values people and relationships with them.[100] Let's say I pay The Times a deposit of $20 this month to get access to its content. But then let's imagine I can earn down my fee next month by bringing value to The Times in ways that help the company make or save money, receiving so many points for:

- coming back often and seeing its ads;
- sharing my demographics and other data with The Times so it can sell higher-value advertising and better target its services to me to increase my use and engagement;
- bringing content — news tips, photos, engaging discussions, assignments in crowdsourced projects — to The Times;
- buying products from or through The Times;
- marketing The Times by recommending its good work on Twitter and Facebook (acknowledging the moral hazard that people may game the system and link just to earn points) or even selling

memberships to my friends (acknowledging the risk that The Times could turn me into a spammer).

If I bring sufficient value to The Times, I get it for free and possibly earn other benefits; if I don't and come just once or twice a month, then perhaps I should no longer be allowed to freeload. Perhaps I should pay (unless, of course, The Times can convert the freeloader into a valued customer).

My point with this illustration: We need to understand that a relationship is an exchange of value. Our users bring value of different sorts and at varying levels. We need to find ways to calculate that value and we need currencies other than just cash to exploit and reward it. The Times can reward valued users with more than content: admission to events; special status in online discussions (because I put my money where my mouth is and converse under my actual identity); special status and thus social capital in real life (why do you think NPR listeners carry public radio tote bags?); and even a voice in some of the decisions of the paper (I know that will make journalists nervous but such a model is being explored on Kickstarter, with members of the public supporting one reporting initiative over another).

These ideas bring us to the edge of patronage, philanthropy, and crowdfunding — from the pledge to an NPR station to the pledge for a journalist's project on Kickstarter:[101] Some people will support the journalism they want to exist. Their reward is not necessarily access. Our motivations could be many: generosity, altruism, activism, justice, credit, social capital, or just warm fuzzies. Journalists — including many of my students before I've had the chance to corrupt them and turn them into capitalists — tend to love this model because it seems so easy and clean (no need to sell advertising, they think) and because it plays to their editorial ego: My work has worth and it deserves this support. But patronage has its issues. First, there simply isn't enough generosity, whether from foundations or individuals, to pay for all the journalism the nation needs. Foundations will warn you that they will not support operations forever; they expect grantees to find other means of sustaining themselves. Second, there is no free lunch; charity often comes with strings. We have seen plenty of cases of fat cats wearing white knights' armor "saving" newspapers only to try to use them as their personal and political bully pulpits. I have watched journalistic not-for-profits forced to deal with the demands of philanthropists and foundations. Before assuming that advertising is corrupting, we would do well to remember that it was advertising that freed newspapers from the ownership and control of political parties.

That said, direct contributions are a potential source of support for the creation of journalistic enterprises as well as their ongoing operation. When venture capitalist John Thornton founded The Texas Tribune, I begged him to use his considerable capitalistic skills to make it a for-profit business instead of a not-for-profit, but he insisted that if Texas could support a ballet company or two, it could support his Texas Tribune. The Knight Foundation leads other media funders in subsidizing the creation of important journalistic experiments and infrastructure (Knight is a funder of my work at CUNY). New platforms such as Patreon enable fans of a lone journalist's work to pay for each piece of work delivered. And in New Jersey, we will experiment with campaigns to allow neighbors to contribute support to their local bloggers.

The Guardian worked for a few years to develop its membership plan. In announcing it, Alan Rusbridger, the paper's editor-in-chief, recounted a discussion with readers at a large Guardian event: "Most readers said they would happily contribute money to the 'cause' of the Guardian — but an overwhelming majority also wanted the journalism to be free, so that it could reach the maximum possible audience. A fair number were happy to be subscribers, but the most hands shot up when asked if they would like to be 'members'."[102] The Guardian offers three levels of membership — friend for free, partner for £15 a month, and patron for £60 a month with varying benefits, featuring discounts and priority booking to events in new space near the paper's London headquarters. I think membership can develop a richer definition around the idea of joining a cause and helping it succeed.

At CUNY, I get to brainstorm new revenue opportunities with our students: Youyoung Lee developed a platform called Gourmeet for people to organize and pay for dinner parties with friends and strangers (if you were to start a newspaper food section today, wouldn't you want to help readers do what they want to do: cook and eat?). Brianne Garcia worked on turning the fundamental marketing relationship on its head, enabling a customer to say what she wants so marketers could come to her and compete for her business. At Informerly, Ranjan Roy and his cofounder are building an impressive business delivering personalized news feeds to executives.[103] They started with customized email newsletters and found that with the right data about users and the right content in return, they could increase the open rate for email newsletters to an astounding 70 percent. At the Tow-Knight Center, we are publishing research on best practices for revenue — advertising products and sales, events, membership, and print — for small-scale sites. Companies old and new, big and small, as well as universities need much more experimentation with revenue and business models built around more than just the tried-and-true: charging readers for access to content and charging advertisers for access to readers. Slate's editor at large David Plotz tweeted 71 ways for digital media to make money and then, in his 72nd tweet, asked, "What did I miss?"[104] I'll ask the same question as we challenge a few more fundamental assumptions about the news business.

THE PRICING PARADOX
OF INFORMATION

In Adam Smith's paradox of value, he wondered why, if water is vital to life and diamonds are not, diamonds are worth so much more than water.[105] The pricing paradox of information presents a similar quandary: If information is so much more valuable to society than entertainment, why is it so hard to build a business — namely, journalism — around selling access to information? Journalism at its most useful is information-rich but information is quickly commodified. Entertainment, on the other hand, is unique and engaging and — for reasons I'll explain in a moment — receives greater legal protection under copyright than information does. We have conflated journalism as an information business with entertainment as an engagement business in large part because both are are built on "stories."

Information is less valuable in the market because it flows freely. Once a bit of information, a fact, appears in a newspaper, it can be repeated and spread, citizen to citizen, TV anchor to audience: "Oyez, oyez, oyez" shouts the town crier. "The king is dead. Long live the king. Pass it on." Information itself cannot and must not be owned. Under copyright law, a creator cannot protect ownership of underlying facts or knowledge, only of their treatment. That is, you cannot copyright the *fact* that the Higgs boson was discovered at CERN in 2012, you can copyright only your *treatment* of that information: your cogent backgrounder or natty graphic that explains WTF a boson is.[106] A well-informed society must protect and celebrate the easy sharing of information even if that does support freeloaders like TV news, which build businesses on the repetition of information others have uncovered. Society cannot find itself in a position in which information is property to be owned, for then the authorities will tell some people — whether they are academics or scientists or students or citizens — what they are not allowed to know because they didn't buy permission to know it. Therein lies a fundamental flaw in the presumption that the public should and will pay for access to information — a fundamental flaw in the business model of journalism. I'm not saying that information wants to be free.[107] I agree that information often is expensive to gather. Instead I am saying that the mission of journalism is to inform society by unlocking and spreading information. Journalism frees information.

Entertainment operates under an entirely different business and legal regime. Entertainment is a unique treatment of knowledge, ideas, and creativity. Its products can be owned and controlled. Entertainment can flourish behind a paywall, protected by copyright (though, of course, digitization of content makes the copying of it without the right to do so easy; I'll explore that matter next). There is only one *Sopranos* and so I happily paid HBO to enjoy its stories. Journalists tend to believe that their work should be treated in the market and by the law like an episode of the *Sopranos* because journalists are storytellers. There's where our confusion lies: In journalism, we came to conflate information and entertainment because we used a common form of both — storytelling — to convey information. Gutenberg's press, the book, the newspaper, the magazine, and the TV show forced us to create a format for filling their pages or minutes and presenting information in the form of a story. We built our business on the presumption that readers were engaged with our storytelling. But let's be honest: Most news — the sewer board hearing, the price of pork bellies, the appointment of a new parks commissioner — isn't inherently entertaining. When we try to make it engaging, we often corrupt our mission. We create tabloid headlines that play up conflict. We look for the edge case that makes a compelling yarn with villain and victim. We turn every political action into a drama — or a horse race, if you prefer — whose ending we want to foreshadow. News — day-to-day, useful, practical, and important news and information — isn't entertainment and does not operate under entertainment's business model.

Mind you, entertainment can be informative and enlightening and news can be engaging and even entertaining. See most any issue of The New Yorker. I bought Michael Lewis' *Flash Boys: A Wall Street Revolt* to be engaged and came away informed. One of our graduates, Samantha Gross, founded a business called Story Tour to take stories to the streets, so storytellers can engage the listeners formerly known as readers where the tales occur.[108] Another graduate, Noah Rosenberg, built Narrative.ly to produce engaging, mixed-media narratives about New York that would each fill a week online.[109] In her latest of many professional incarnations, Tina Brown promises to develop what she calls live journalism: "summits, salons, flash forums, and debates," all forms of informative entertainment.[110] And I will happily sell you my previous books.[111] Each of us is competing for customers' attention and dollars with other forms of media and entertainment: novels, movies, TV, music, games, sports. Just because news can occasionally be entertaining and be sold as a product doesn't mean the workaday stories of the Podunk Daily Disgrace should be sold like a movie. This confusion about the lines between information and entertainment — their business models, value propositions, and legal status — has contributed to the will to build paywalls. If Tony Soprano can have a wall, then why can't Tom Friedman? Just because information and entertainment have shared a format — the story — doesn't mean they are in the same business. Useful information is still the key asset we offer in news and as I explored in the second part of this essay, we can now offer it in forms besides the story.

I have argued that journalism should remake itself as a service that helps people accomplish goals rather than as a production line that makes content to fill products that can be sold. So what would a business built on information as service look like? You might well argue to me that customers *do* pay for services. I pay my plumber to install my sink. If a journalist informs me, shouldn't I pay her? Some people do pay for information: the customers of Bloomberg or Thomson Reuters, for example. Tom Glocer, former head of Thomson Reuters, used to say that the information his company sold was most valuable in its first three milliseconds of life — which happens to be the basis of the story Michael Lewis tells in *Flash Boys*. Everything else that Thomson Reuters produces from that information — from its wire service to its web site — is a byproduct worth fractionally less. This tells us that if you have information that is uniquely valuable to a customer and you can deliver it before anyone else, you can charge for access to it. But what you're selling then isn't so much information as speed. Here we face the factor of time in the pricing paradox of information: The more valuable the information, the faster it will spread and the faster it spreads, the less valuable it becomes. Where does this leave us? It leaves us with the need to consider new ways to conceive of media, audience, content, and intellectual property.

THE LINK ECONOMY
AND CREDITRIGHT

There have long been two creations of value in media: the creation of content, yes, but also the creation of a public — an audience — for it. In legacy news media, the two were usually attached: the creator and the distributor were one in a vertically integrated enterprise (read: a publication). We often debated whether content or distribution was king. The answer didn't much matter because they were inseparable; they shared the throne. Now these two tasks are — like so much else online — unbundled. Anyone can make content. Anyone can distribute content: its creator (inside or outside an institution), a reader who recommends it, an aggregator or curator who collects it, a search engine that points to it.

Media people tend to believe that content has intrinsic value — that is why they say people *should* pay for it and why some object when Google quotes snippets from it. But in an ecosystem of links online, new economics are in force. Online, content with no links has no value because it has no audience. Content gains value as it gains links. That formula was the key insight behind Google: that links to content are a signal of its value; thus, the more links to a page from sites that themselves have more links, the more useful, relevant, or valuable that content is likely to be.

The problem for us in the media industry is that we have no marketplace to value the gathering of links and audiences. Our systems are still built primarily around extracting the value of content: paying creators to make it; buying or subscribing to publications that contain it; or syndicating it from one publication to the next. These models are being made obsolete. Huffington Post and Twitter can get thousands of writers — including me — to make content for free because it brings us audience and attention. Selling content is difficult when you compete against others who offer content for free. And syndication is all but outmoded, for why should I buy a piece of content if instead I can link to it for nothing?[112]

Consider an alternative to syndication. I'll call it reverse syndication. Instead of selling my content to you, what say I give it to you for free? Better yet, I pay you to publish it on your site. The condition: I get to put my ad on the content. I will pay you a share of what I earn from that ad based on how much audience you bring me. That model values the creation of the audience. When The New York Times complains about Huffington Post summarizing its articles, perhaps The Times would be better off offering Huffington Post this deal: Take our stories but keep them intact with Times branding, advertising, and links. We'll give you a share of what we earn for each story based on the size — and perhaps quality, as measured in attention and demographics — of the audience you bring to it.

For that matter, why should media always force our readers to come to us? Why shouldn't our content go to them? Before Gutenberg's press, scholars had to travel to books; after Gutenberg, the books traveled to the scholars. We've long had home delivery for newspapers, magazines, and TV, so why not extend that service to content on the web? For years, I had wished for a means to make articles and blog posts embeddable on other sites, just like YouTube videos. If content could travel with its business model attached, we could set it free to travel across the web, gathering recommendations and audience and value as it goes, and thus ending at least part of the fight over the question of whether aggregation is theft. I was about to build a demonstration of the embeddable article at CUNY when Debbie Galant, head of the New Jersey News Commons, did what the author of a book about Google should have thought to do: She searched Google for "embeddable article" and up came Repost.us, already created by entrepreneur and technologist John Pettitt. Repost very cleverly allowed embeddable articles to travel with the creator's own brand, advertising, analytics, and links. So if you like something on my blog, rather than just quoting and linking to it, you could embed the entire post on your own site with my complete text, my brand, my advertising, and links back to my site. Thus you get free content and I get more audience.

In early experience with partners including The Christian Science Monitor and Agence France-Presse, Pettitt discovered two surprising facts about embedding: First, he found that the overlap in audience between a creator's and an embedder's sites generally ran between 2 and 5 percent. That is to say, the embedders brought a mostly new audience to the creator's content. Second, you might think that the click-through from an embedded article would be nil because the reader has been sated, having consumed the entire piece. Instead, Pettitt found that click-through ran amazingly high: 5 to 7 percent — and these were highly qualified clicks of people who knew what they were going to get on the other side of a link, not just drive-bys from search engines or Facebook. In New Jersey, the News Commons used Repost as the basis of a content- and audience-sharing network among dozens of sites big and small in the state's new ecosystem. The big site, NJ.com, brought new and sizable audience to smaller sites' content — for example, the government reporting of NJ Spotlight. NJ.com also made its articles available for smaller sites to use. Each creator's ads traveled with its content — though that wasn't necessarily optimal, because an ad for a North Jersey hairdresser wouldn't perform terribly well with South Jersey readers brought in through embedding. So my next ambition was to create an ad network to maximize the value of this traffic.

But then, in mid-2014, Repost shut down its service. So much for a happy ending to my quest for a network built on the value of the link economy. A key factor in its failure: Repost could find many sites willing and eager to make their content embeddable. It didn't find enough sites to embed the content. As an evangelist for the link economy, I should have seen the problem sooner: We were still valuing the creation of content over the creation of audiences. Content makers fared well in the transactions Repost enabled: They got more audience for their content and ads, and more revenue as a result. But the embedders got nothing aside from the free use of content — content that was just a link away anyway. I now see that we should have arranged to pay the embedders a share of the revenue, thus valuing their creation of audiences. My duh. There's a happier ending, though: A competitor called iCopyright is providing New Jersey's network with its embedder, repubHub, which also enables content sales.[113] And I was oddly gratified to see some members of the ecosystem who had to be dragged into the embedding network screaming louder when it went away. The New Jersey model proves that embedding works as the basis of a network.

Our ultimate problem in media is that we do not have sufficient technical and legal frameworks for alternate business models. Copyright is built for one model: the Gutenberg-era notion that creativity equals content that can be bought and sold as intellectual property. What of the other models the internet now enables? I have been part of a project at the World Economic Forum that has been seeking to update our understanding of how to support creativity and to move past the bitter and unproductive fight over copyright and the net. That fight played itself out in the battle that defeated SOPA and

PIPA — proposed laws meant to punish copyright violators online — as a war of Northern California vs. Southern California, Silicon Valley vs. Hollywood. Hollywood's side: People who download our content without buying it or who remix it without our permission — and the platforms that facilitate these behaviors — are stealing from us and must be stopped and punished. Silicon Valley's: Those people are your fans who are bringing value to you by sending you audiences and by contributing their creativity, and you'd be wise to build your businesses around making it easier, not harder, for them to get and share your content when and how they want it. Around and around this argument has gone — like the fight over paywalls — arriving nowhere. It has been a clash of eras, of worldviews and economies.

The Forum stepped in to convene a series of discussions in New York, London, Djakarta, San Francisco, and Davos (some of which I moderated) to try to get a diverse set of constituents — creators, publishers, studios, platforms, technologists, lawyers, academics, and government officials — to break the rancorous deadlock of the copyright fight and find common ground to move forward. It informed these discussions with research on audience behaviors and attitudes in the U.K. and Indonesia as study markets, exposing widely divergent views and norms. For example, when given the statement "anything I download from the internet should be free," only 17 percent in the U.K. agreed but 54 percent in Indonesia agreed. To my surprise, the discussions have made progress. In private, media moguls would concede that copyright was outmoded and technologists would admit that their systems were inadequate. Together, they heard creative artists describe new models they used to support themselves, some wanting their work to spread widely so they could sell tickets to events, find patrons to volunteer support, or gather data about their fans and their behavior to understand them better and build richer relationships with them. And so, we came to agree that we need new technological and legal frameworks flexible enough to enable multiple models to support creativity.

I call this creditright. We need a means to attach credit to content for those who contribute value to it so that each constituent has the opportunity to negotiate and extract value along the chain, so that each can gain permission to take part in the chain, and so that behaviors that benefit others in the chain can be rewarded and encouraged. A scenario from outside news: Imagine you are a songwriter. You hear a street poet and her words inspire you to write a song about her, quoting her in the piece. You go to a crowdfunding platform — Kickstarter, Indiegogo, or Patreon — to raise money for you to go into the studio and perform and distribute your song. Another songwriter comes along and remixes it, making a new version and also sampling from others' songs. Both end up on YouTube and Soundcloud, on iTunes and Google Play. Audience members discover and share the songs. A particularly popular artist shares the remixed version on Twitter and Facebook and it explodes. A label has one of its stars record it. The star appears on TV performing it. A movie studio includes that song in a soundtrack. There are many constituents in that process: the subject, the songwriter, the patrons, the fans, the remixer, the distributor, the label, the star, the show, the studio, and the platforms. Each contributed value. Each may want to recognize value — but not all will want cash. There are other currencies in play: The poet may want credit and fame; the songwriter may want to sell concert tickets; the patrons may want social capital for discovering and supporting a new artist; the remixer may want permission to remix; the platforms may want a cut of sales or of subscription revenue; the show may want audience and advertising; the studio will want a return on its investment and risk. If we transferred this scenario to news, a publisher may want data about users' interests and behaviors from others in a chain of links to better serve them with more relevant content and to receive greater engagement in return. The publisher may want demographic data about users to serve them more valuable advertising. Or the publisher may want to reward some contributors to a collaborative project for their work and others for their recommendations and promotion.

German news publishers have fought Google in courts and legislatures as well as media and political forums, seeking a share of Google's revenue in the belief that Google steals their content when it quotes from them in the listings it uses to send publishers billions of clicks a month. Relying on on copyright, they lobbied government to enact a new law — a *Leistungsschutzrecht* or ancillary copyright — to demand payment. I have argued with these publishers that Google will not — and should not — pay them. Google is creating value for them with the audience it sends their way. Instead, I've suggested they would be wiser to seek another currency from Google: data about the users, helping build better services for readers and advertisers and thus better businesses. I also fear that the Germans — and Spanish politicians who proposed a law to in essence tax links — will undermine the very essence of the web just to protect entrenched, legacy institutions.

What system will do all that we need in a new universe of digital creativity? We will need a way to attach metadata to content, recording and revealing its source and the contributions of others in the chain of continuing creation and distribution. We need a marketplace to measure and value their contributions and a means to negotiate rewards and permissions. We need payment structures to handle multiple currencies: data as well as money. And we need a legal framework to allow the flexible exploration of new models, some of which we cannot yet imagine. It so happens that I am writing this on the plane as I head to moderate another meeting the Forum has convened in San Francisco to discuss these questions. We won't solve these problems and design these systems in an hour. It took more than 150 years after the invention of the press before the Statute of Anne — that is, copyright — was enacted. At that time some governments awarded licenses to sanctioned monopolies for the right to use the press in an attempt to limit publishing's power and disruption. It took many more years for society to develop principles of free speech to balance the economic and political interests of those who would attempt to control a new tool of speech. And, of course, even with laws governing copyright, fair use, fair comment, censorship, and speech, we are still fighting over all these issues. As Harvard Law School Professor Lawrence Lessig has said, the right to fair use is the right to hire a copyright attorney.

What this process needs is first the willingness to question our Gutenberg-age models and assumptions, valuing not just content as a commodity that fills publications but also valuing the people who contribute to a creative process and the gathering of those people, formerly known as an audience. Second, it requires discussion, such as those organized and informed by the World Economic Forum, which is uniquely suited to convene many constituents to serious consideration of new opportunities. And finally, it demands experiments, such as John Pettitt's Repost.us. Pettitt did a great job thinking through a myriad of copyright issues (e.g., whether a news site had the right to redistribute a wire photo that accompanied a story) and technical issues (e.g., how to make an embedded article look compatible with the embedder's site). But he may not have grappled sufficiently with the human matter of motivating people to embed others' content (that is, paying them). Nonetheless, Pettitt contributed valuable ideas, data, and lessons to the process of rethinking the notions of content, copyright, and intellectual property.

The link — the insight of Sir Tim Berners-Lee, the Gutenberg of our age — changes media at such an atomic level that it is impossible to believe we can continue to operate under old business models, old legal frameworks, old metrics, and old technologies. We must reimagine the business of media and news from the first penny, asking where value is created, who contributes to it, where it resides, and how to extract it. Creditright is one model for this reimagining. It is hardly a unified theory. And it would be foolhardy to think that we know enough yet to be able to develop complete theories. This is why I started this essay urging us all to rethink the relationships journalists and media have with the public they serve in the age of the link. It is why I next challenged us to rethink the possible forms of the services we provide. Only then, after much exploration and experimentation, can we discover our business models. I suggest we start not by following the money but by following the value. Thus, we need new measures of value.

METRICS

We get what we measure and we are measuring the wrong things in media. Our old, mass-media metrics of reach and frequency — translated into their digital equivalents: unique users and pageviews — turn out to be profoundly corrupting. They drive media outlets to do anything to bulk up their numbers, prioritizing quantity over quality of service and engagement and motivating some to game the system with dark-hat search-engine optimization and click bait, not to mention click fraud. Now I don't mean to suggest that we from legacy media were pure as arctic ice. I worked for the New York Daily News. I wrote tabloid headlines to entice readers to buy my newspaper — coin bait rather than click bait. But online, small temptations can turn into systems of corruption at scale. Three illustrations:

About.com was the first media company built for the Google age. It produced the answers to questions commonly asked in Google searches. Thus its content rose up high in Google search, getting it huge traffic from Google as well as highly relevant Google ads and millions of dollars a year in revenue. That was a virtuous circle until Demand Media and other so-called content farms came along to game the system, creating a platform to pay writers with a few spare minutes the minimum possible to make content that was barely good enough but would still rise in search, attracting easy audience and easy advertising. Google ended that gravy train — throwing

About.com's baby out with Demand Media's dirty bathwater — to protect the quality of its search results.

Buzzfeed and Upworthy perfected the listicle and the grabby headline (*You won't believe what happened next but it will change your life!*) to manipulate not Google's search algorithms but instead us, enticing people to share and "like" their content. But that bubble, too, is set to burst as Chartbeat found that people share before they read — if they ever read at all.[114] There's a reason that Huffington Post, for example, displays links to share — to Facebook, Twitter, Reddit, StumbleUpon, Tumblr, Google+, and email — right next to its headlines rather than at the bottom of its posts. Sharing a link turns out not to be an indication of engagement — as in, "they liked my story so much they had to share it with their friends." Sharing pumps up mentions and maybe unique users and pageviews but not attention. So what good is it?

Finally, consider the newspapers that got so good at SEO and social links (not to mention the occasional and unpredictable burst of pageviews that comes from a link by Drudge) that they exploded their traffic but ended up with large proportions of users from outside their markets. That distant traffic is next to worthless — as I mentioned earlier, an in-market user can be worth 20 times what an out-of-market user is worth to a news site that has only in-market advertising sales. But most newspapers I know got caught in an egotistical traffic game: size for the sake of size and bragging rights.

These examples of the corrupting nature of unique users and pageviews make the case to build a new set of metrics upon which to build news and media businesses.

The Demand Media example argues for starting with basic engagement metrics: not how many people glance off a site and then disappear like a meteor shower hitting the atmosphere, but how many people return, how often, and how long they stay and engage.

The interactivity of online allows for many more acts and measures of engagement, some of which I listed earlier in my reverse-pay-meter scenario: from joining in a discussion to contributing content to collaborating in the work of a site.

The case of shared and liked links producing little engagement and value augers for switching to attention metrics. Chartbeat's Tony Haile has argued convincingly that attention is a much more productive measure of media value than traffic. I told how Medium and FT.com plan to charge advertisers for the total attention minutes they get instead of mere impressions. Bonus: TV advertising is also sold on time and advertisers love buying TV, so we can hope that selling time online will help draw dollars away from TV to online news ventures.

And my newspaper example is evidence of the need to shift to relationship metrics: How many people do you know? What do you know about them? (Start with finding out whether they live in your market.) What reasons did you give them to reveal themselves to you? What relevance and value did you return to them for the data they shared? What value were you able to recognize as a result? What do you know about the interrelationships of people inside your community? How can you help them to better connect with each other, sharing knowledge, helping, and transacting with each other? What do you know about their behavior because you have a relationship with them? How does that knowledge drive not only usage, engagement, and loyalty but also revenue? What more do you know about their demographics and buying behavior because you've built trusted relationships and how will that increase the value of what you sell to advertisers? If the relationship strategy offers an opportunity to rethink journalism as a service business that builds real and lasting value, we need to measure the things that will drive that strategy.

In the long run, attention, engagement, demographic, behavioral, and relationship metrics will beat mere mass measures. That's because advertisers are waking up to realize that they, too, must operate by such new measurements. But all the metrics I have listed so far still tend to be mediacentric: How many people read, returned to, spent time with, liked, or interacted with *us* and *our* stuff?

There is a richer set of metrics that matter to the mission of journalism — metrics around impact and accomplishment. These metrics must start not with us but with the people we serve. They must measure whether *they* meet *their* needs and accomplish *their* goals. Thus journalism built around impact doesn't start with producing media's content; it starts with listening to the public's wants, needs, and goals so we can measure our success ultimately against whether those goals are achieved. (Therein lies the heart of our rationale for starting a new degree at CUNY in social journalism, a journalism built first on listening to and understanding and then serving a community; more on that in the afterword.)

Impact is terribly difficult to measure. It cannot easily be reduced to a number in a chart. But that is precisely why we should pursue these measures, because they force us to see people as individuals again; they force us to listen. Columbia University scholar James Carey argued that media were corrupted by the desire to reduce people to mere numbers — pro vs. anti, red vs. blue — as exemplified by the public-opinion poll. Polling, he said, "was an attempt to simulate public opinion in order to prevent an authentic public opinion from forming."[115] His alternative: conversation with the public. "I believe we must begin with the primacy of conversation," Carey wrote. "It implies social arrangements less hierarchical and more egalitarian than its alternatives." Yes, we have conversations online now, plenty of conversation in bottomless comments sections under our articles. But those comments are still mediacentric, reacting to the content *we* produce. No, the proper conversation journalists should have must start with the public. These conversations must start not with us speaking but with us listening. Thus I come to better understand my friend Jay Rosen's interpretation of Carey's admonitions to journalists: "The press does not 'inform' the public," Rosen said. "It is 'the public' that ought to inform the press. The true subject matter of journalism is the conversation the public is having with itself."

Now I return to amend the relationship metrics I proposed above: How many people have we met — where possible, face-to-face? How rich and informative were our conversations with them? How well do we understand them and their communities? How well have we heard or discerned their needs and goals? *That* is the starting point.

Only then, only when we have listened well, can we ask the next questions: What does an individual or a community need to accomplish its goals? How can we help? Is it information you need? How can we help you share what you already know? If what you need is not known, then how can we bring reporting to the task? Is it understanding you need? Then how can we bring explanation and context or education? Is it functionality you need? Do we have the skills to implement or build that? Is it organization you need? Can we help convene a community to deliberate and accomplish its goals?

Only after we have contributed to a community's efforts to reach its own goals can we begin to think of measuring success — that is, impact. Chalkbeat, a beat business that covers schools in a scattering of cities across America, asks whether its communities have improved their schools. Founder and CEO Elizabeth Green emphasizes that Chalkbeat does not say how that should be done or even how that should be measured (for its users will debate long and hard about, say, the efficacy of testing as a metric of educational quality). But Chalkbeat can listen to whether the community says its schools are better. The investigative reporting enterprise ProPublica asks whether corruption is reduced and thus equality enhanced. A local blog might ask whether neighbors see improvements in the quality of life in their communities.

These questions are not easily answered — if at all — with numbers. The answers are by their nature qualitative and made up of signals that can be gathered in ongoing conversations. That may seem like a quixotic equation that will frustrate an industry and its financial supporters — whether investors or philanthropists — accustomed to running the business according to easy numbers. But the more valuable journalism and the services it provides are to communities, the more valuable those enterprises will be. That is an article of faith that guides Silicon Valley startups: Start with making yourself useful and value will follow. If it's good enough for them. . . .

CAPITAL: INVESTMENT IN THE FUTURE

It took a half-century after Gutenberg's invention of the press for the book to take on the form we know today. It took a full century, according to Gutenberg scholar Elizabeth Eisenstein, for the book's impact on society to be fully realized.[116] I'm astounded that it took 150 years — and the development of postal networks — before someone thought to use the press to print the first newspaper, the Strasbourg Relation, in 1605.[117] "The newspaper, as it turned out, would have a difficult birth," writes Andrew Pettegree in *The Invention of News: How The World Came to Know About Itself.* "Many of the first newspapers struggled to make money, and swiftly closed. . . . [I]t would be well over a hundred years from the foundation of the first newspaper before it became an everyday part of life."[118] In *The Transformation of the World: A Global History of the Nineteenth Century*, Jürgen Osterhammel adds: "Not until four centuries after Gutenberg did the printed news media enter the daily lives of more than a tiny educated stratum of society."[119] The term "journalism" did not even come into use until the year 1833.[120]

In the development of the internet and of news in its age, we are — as I write this — only two decades past the introduction of the commercial browser and web in 1994. In Gutenberg years, this is 1470. I doubt we can yet imagine how society will inform itself. We have been too busy trying to save the news we knew to invent what news will be. As far as the newspaper was from the town crier and the balladeer, so will news of the future likely look unrecognizable to us today. There is much innovation, invention, development, risk, and failure yet to come. I am more concerned about funding that work than keeping afloat the ongoing operations of legacy news organizations, for it's that investment that will build the future.

I teach my entrepreneurial journalism students that Gutenberg was the first technology entrepreneur. He had to solve a complex matrix of technology challenges. His crucial invention was the hand-held mold that enabled him to manufacture fonts with precision and speed at scale. He concocted the right metallurgy — lead, tin, and antimony — so each molded letter would cool quickly and aid that speed and scale. He had to find paper, imported from Italy, of just the right thickness to take impressions on both sides. He experimented with the proper amount of moisture on the paper to help the ink — which he also formulated — set with the rich blackness we can still see on his pages today. While working on what were for him beta products — a grammar book — to perfect his process, he operated with Jobsian secrecy to prevent others from stealing his invention. To bring his idea to reality and to market, Gutenberg needed capital. He had to build all that technology, acquire space in Mainz, heat it, pay workmen, and acquire considerable stocks of paper and metal. He went to one Johann Fust to get funds for what Gutenberg interpreted to be equity and Fust took to be a loan. Just as Gutenberg's Bibles were to come off the press and just as he was finally to benefit from his cash flow, Fust called the loan. They ended up in a court fight, which Gutenberg lost, along with his primary printing plant and most of his business. After I told this tale in a Kindle Single, *Gutenberg the Geek*,[121] a waggish geek I know summed up the moral of the story with this cringeworthy question: "Would you rather be first or Fust?"

Media startups face similar issues of investment capital and cash flow; that's why I teach Gutenberg as a case. Every term with my students, I draw on the whiteboard a simplistic chart with what I call the C.A.R rule: A media business starts with nothing and must build its *content* until it has enough of a critical mass of value to gather an *audience* until it has enough of a critical mass of people to attract advertising *revenue*. Content. Audience. Revenue. Until that point is reached, the media business needs investment — cash and sweat equity — sufficient to subsidize its birth. Opening a bakery, on the other hand, one can start earning cash with the first cronut.

Where will the innovation we require come from? It will spring from many levels: from startups that come from classrooms and garages, from the scattered technological Valleys, and, I hope, from some brave legacy companies and their owners. I refuse to give up on the incumbents, though many of my friends in the industry say I should. The old institutions do have assets: cash flow (though in some cases that's trickling), brand recognition (though that will be fleeting as younger people move through the population python), a measure of trust (though not nearly as much as journalists would like to think), experience (though that can also mean habits that are hard to break), infrastructure (though that can be an economic albatross around their necks), and a system of ethics and standards (isn't that what defines journalism in the end?). I suppose another asset is desperation and we know whose child that is. Some have given up. The Graham family, who had nurtured, sustained, supported, and protected the Washington Post from 1933 to 2013, surrendered and sold to Jeff Bezos (who, I pray, will bring his expertise in relationships to the enterprise). The Philadelphia Inquirer, once a magnet for Pulitzer Prizes, went through multiple owners and torture of such a sadistic scale that I cannot see it ever recovering. A number of media conglomerates built on a foundation of news spun off their old news and print divisions to keep those financial cooties away from what had become their core business; that is, separating struggling information businesses from profitable entertainment businesses — Scripps in 2007, Belo in 2008, News Corp. in 2013, Tribune Company in 2014, Time-Warner in 2014, Gannett in 2014. Unlike many of these owners and to his credit, Rupert Murdoch did not saddle his legacy spinoff with debt; his new News Corp. started its life with no debt and $2.6 billion in cash[122] — enough to fund considerable innovation.

I have worked with a number of legacy companies during this period, this age of disruption. I was an executive at Advance Publications for a dozen years beginning the month before the release of the commercial browser in 1994. After leaving to teach, I continued working with them on projects in Michigan and New Jersey that resulted in the disbanding of newspaper companies and the formation of new digital companies. Advance reduced frequency of some of its papers to reduce costs. It truly made the transition to digital first when its papers became byproducts produced by small staffs drawing from the digital work being done at the heart of its new online operations. I've advised the Guardian starting after it installed what editor-in-chief Alan Rusbridger acknowledged were its last presses[123] and as it began to reimagine itself as a digital enterprise. The Guardian sold assets to build its endowment to over $1 billion and it continues to innovate and grow audience as an international brand, though it also chooses to invest and forego profit. I was on the board of advisers of at Digital First Media as its CEO, Paton, merged together, rethought, and restructured two large and suffering newspaper companies into one more efficient, more digital corporation — America's second largest chain — that could finally bring returns for its hedge-fund owners. In 2014, to save money, Digital First shut down its centralized hub of innovation, called Project Thunderdome. None of these tales culminates in what journalists would consider a happy ending: more money for more journalists. Each company lost many jobs along the way. Blame me as an adviser, if you will, for not finding the fairy-tale ending. But in spots, I do see progress.

Across many industries, the old, vertically integrated companies operating inside oligopolies are being challenged and replaced by ecosystems built on three layers: *platforms* at the base that make it possible for *entrepreneurial* ventures to start and run with less capital and less risk, and *networks* that bring those ventures to critical mass for sharing resources. To look at an ecosystem such as New Jersey, the *platforms* — Google, WordPress, Twitter, Facebook, et al — make it possible for a broad array of *entrepreneurial* ventures to exist — as local blogs or beat businesses, mostly — and now they are coming together in *networks* to share content, audience, advertising, technology, training, and other services. Today, in these new ecosystems, the platforms gather the scale and the largest share of profit but as the ecosystem develops, its other members will gain strength. Each of these layers is an opportunity for innovation, growth, and investment.

News' rebirth requires investment at every level: to get beat businesses off the ground and multiplying to scale (tens of thousands of dollars each); to build new and larger-scale news enterprises (low millions of dollars); to innovate and experiment in and rebuild the legacy news companies that survive (tens of millions of dollars each); and to build the technologies that will facilitate the development of new forms of news (anywhere from from a few thousand dollars in a Kickstarter campaign to hundreds of millions for the next Twitter or Google). Where will this money come from? We don't have enough friends-and-family money and enough charitable and philanthropic dollars to support all that needs to be done. Private equity and hedge funds will not have the long-term perspective needed for this work and the stock market certainly does not. Venture capital? When I visit

VCs in Silicon Valley or Alley and argue that there are opportunities in the future of news and journalism, I am often met with polite, sad smiles. Yes, some say, you have opportunities, but not as worthy as those from technology companies. We don't invest in content, they say. Venture capital is predicated on earning huge returns building disruptive technological platforms that scale. Journalism — content — doesn't scale. They're right. This is one reason why I think we must get out of the business of primarily making content and get into the business of building, adapting, or distributing platforms that enable people to share their own information, adding journalistic value to that process (sometimes with content). This is the relationship strategy. I also believe that in many areas — especially local news — scale will come not from the top-down (à la Patch) but instead from the bottom up with the messy, disorganized proliferation of beat businesses: free-agent-nation, mom-or-pop news bakeries. I do not imagine — and do not want — to think that a single behemoth, a Google or Facebook or (heaven help us) a Comcast or Verizon of news, will suddenly rise up to meet all our journalistic and information needs. Venture capital has indeed funded some media ventures, like Buzz-Feed, Business Insider, Vox Media, and Vice. Some of these are transitional companies that cleverly exploit opportunities and vulnerabilities in the present marketplace — search-engine optimization or social optimization, for example — but still largely operate under the old, mass-media economics of volume.

When the new dean at my journalism school, Sarah Bartlett, and I met with a series of technology CEOs and investors in Silicon Valley, I urged them not to give journalism their pity and charity. Instead, we told them we need their innovation and investment and a transfer of skills from the West Coast to the East Coast. We need them to build platforms that enable an informed society. We need them to reinvent advertising (and, I hope, find a role for media in that).[124] We need them to invest their fortunes in the future of news.

Journalist and entrepreneur Steve Waldman, founder of Beliefnet and author of a Federal Communications Commission report on the future of news,[125] has argued for some time that we need a new pool of capital for smaller, less-scalable, and — let's be honest — less-profitable news ventures. Those who care about the future of news — including foundations — would do well to invest in beat businesses to get them over that C.A.R hump, in larger news enterprises that still won't be large enough to attract venture capital, in new technology-based companies related to news, and in new ventures even from legacy media companies.

Waldman as well as the Knight Foundation also proposed making it easier for news organizations to get not-for-profit status with the IRS. You have probably noted that I have devoted little to no attention in this essay to not-for-profit news organizations. They play a critical role in our news ecosystem, especially as so many legacy institutions suffer. But I want to caution that not-for-profit news, charity, and philanthropy are not our salvation. Often, students arrive in our entrepreneurial journalism class at CUNY thinking that if their ventures are not-for-profit, they needn't worry about advertising, revenue, profitability, and all those slightly distasteful pursuits that I teach. But, of course, they still must be profitable; whether they put that profit back into the enterprise or into equity-holders' pockets is mostly a distinction of tax status and ownership. This is why I insist that our students' businesses in CUNY's entrepreneurial journalism program be for-profit, because it is the higher business discipline, the better lesson for them. Most times, I succeed at converting them. Once they leave, it's up to them whether they want to run a not-for-profit business, but then I point them to role models like the head of WNYC public radio in New York, Laura Walker, who is a brilliant businesswoman and tough business negotiator. She most certainly runs WNYC as a business, and a good one. Not all not-for-profit news enterprises operate like hers, though. I see too many not-for-profit news organizations devoting too little attention to their own sustainability, investing nothing in raising the revenue they need to keep their good work going and betting their futures on the hope that God or foundations will provide. Not-for-profit news organizations need to exist in a news ecosystem to do those things the market will not do, to cover the broccoli news that matters but won't necessarily attract sizable audience, to patiently dog the stories that need dogging, and to experiment. Organizations such as WNYC, NPR, ProPublica, The Texas Tribune, Chalkbeat, and the Center for Investigative Reporting do that.

There is a role for philanthropy in the development of a future for news. I do not want their charity to interfere in the market and support that which should be sustainable on its own. I do want them to help support the exploration of new journalistic models, technologies, infrastructure, and ventures as well as business models. They can provide patient capital to fund aggressive attempts to explore new relationships, forms, and models for news. What about government support of news? I see danger in government intervention in speech — in journalism — especially in the United States, where it inevitably leads to political pressure and conflict. In Europe and other countries, I have argued that public media already supported by mandatory fees (read: taxes) should become a supporter of the best of market media and an open-source laboratory for innovation in news. Universities, too, should play a role, not only by training tomorrow's journalists and entrepreneurs and retraining today's but also by creating laboratories where innovators can build and explore.

At the start of this essay, I said I would not and could not predict the future of news. But I will make a few bets. Given (1) the strategic straits of large, legacy news companies and (2) the negative attitude toward news as a business held by sources of capital — VCs and the market — and (3) the necessity of inefficient human effort in journalism, I will bet that news will no longer be the domain of vertically integrated corporations. Instead, news will come from distributed ecosystems of specialized enterprises of various sizes, business models, and motives. News will be messy and uneven for sometime to come. But there will be a constantly growing demand for news and information. And now that the public has more means of sharing information, there will also be more sources of news. So I will bet that there will more need and opportunities for journalists. If I didn't believe that, I shouldn't be teaching in a journalism school.

Beside that rather safe bet, I can only make recommendations. I believe journalism should recast itself not as a mass medium or a content producer but as a service built on a foundation of engaged and collaborative relationships with individuals and communities in the public. Journalists should listen first, helping the people they serve meet their own needs and goals. Journalists should question the assumptions and orthodoxies, the culture and organization that arose from their Gutenberg- and industrial-era means of production and distribution and take advantage of the many new opportunities geeks have given them to meet their mission of informing society in better ways.

From a business perspective, legacy news companies need to finish cutting and build their digital futures now. I believe any news enterprise — small or large, new or old, profit or not-for-profit — will benefit from a relationship strategy based on value over volume for both users and advertisers. I wish that every constituent and layer in the new news ecosystem — news organizations of every description, advertisers and their agencies, universities, foundations, and civil society — would invest in innovation to find new futures for news.

I've given you one view: mine. In the beginning of this essay, I asked you to share yours. What futures do you imagine for news? Building the future of journalism requires both urgency and patience. There is no time to waste to recognize the disruption that is upon us, to question old assumptions, to cast off obsolete ways and their costs, to find and exploit new opportunities to better serve our public, and to find new sources of revenue. We also require patience so we have the time to experiment and to fail. We need to support the work of innovators who are not burdened with the assumptions of my generation, who will define news in ways we cannot yet imagine. Their inventions may shock and surprise us — until, like the book and the newspaper, they seem to be such self-evident products of their era. Remember, this is 1470 in Gutenberg years.

Now I return to my friend John Paton, with whom I began this part of the essay. John is controversial because he tries to be. He shakes up people in this industry because they need to be shaken up. Some say he promised too much. Perhaps he did. Or perhaps they put too much hope in him when his time was necessarily limited. Paton did precisely what his hedge-fund investors expected him to do: increase the value of what they saw as troubled assets and we see as treasured institutions of news. He accomplished more as well: bringing a new culture, new expectations, new methods, and even new hope to his newspapers. Then he asked what would come next. But he did not have the patient capital that could get him there. The hedge funds put the company up for sale in 2014. As a colleague of mine observed: Paton was not the Messiah. He was more Moses. He got his newspapers through the desert, making them more digital and sustainable. But he and his owners were not destined to reach the Promised Land. That responsibility and privilege will fall to my students and perhaps to their children: to invent the future of news. That is why I teach, to watch and perhaps help them do that.

AFTERWORD

A NOTE ON JOURNALISM EDUCATION

These three areas of exploration — relationships, forms, and models — play themselves out in the curriculum and programs at the CUNY Graduate School of Journalism in various ways. I offer a description of the areas in which I work as an example of a few ways in which one school is trying to work in this age of change.

To begin with business models: When the school opened its doors in 2006, we offered a course in entrepreneurial journalism. It was really just my pedagogical ploy to teach journalism students the business of journalism in the belief that — especially now — we must produce more responsible stewards of the trade. Having each student build a plan for a new enterprise was a device to have students explore the dynamics of the business and how to sustain it: how news organizations must build a product and an audience before they will have the critical mass necessary to garner advertising revenue; how Google had disrupted the advertising business by exploiting an abundance rather than controlling a scarcity; how much journalism costs. At the start of every term, we list on the whiteboard the questions that most every startup — from Gutenberg on — needs to answer. The students must prepare a plan with:

- An elevator pitch. If you can't succinctly describe your business to customers, users, employees, and investors, then you don't yet know what it is.

- Problem statement. What problem will your business solve? I don't care what you want to do, I tell students. I care what the people out there (dramatically pointing finger at window) *need* you to do. That is why their first assignment is to go interview those people, not about the students' ideas but about the users' needs.

- Market analysis. Who are your customers? How large is your market? What ties them together? Where do you find them?

- Competitive analysis. Often students will say they have no competitors. But, of course, they do. Competitors offer startups the opportunity to improve on what they do and to learn from their mistakes.

- Product or service plan. What is this thing you're offering? What does it do for users? How does it work? What does it look like?

- Revenue plan. This is usually advertising — and we spend more than one class each term on how advertising works today. It can include other revenue streams, of course, depending on the business.

- Marketing plan. How will people find your service? Saying "it will be viral" is not sufficient.

- Operations plan. What will your costs be as a minimally viable product and as a sustainable business? What are your staffing and technology needs?

- Launch plan. No longer does a product need to come out fully birthed. Now it can start with one feature and grow from there.

- Capital needs. If you have a rich uncle or an investor, what are you asking for? What will those funds pay for?

I was fortunate from the start to receive a grant from the MacArthur Foundation that allowed us to give up to $50,000 per year in seed money to students' businesses as juried by a group of entrepreneurs, journalists, publishers, investors, and technologists. Money can be a much better motivator than grades. Of course, it also can be corrupting. I learned many lessons in those early classes: First, the awards of money tended to overemphasize the theatrics of the final presentations in students' minds. Second, juries sometimes compromise on safer choices. Third, giving money to students with nothing more than a plan is like throwing a hothouse orchid onto Times Square and expecting passers-by to water it. They need much more ongoing mentoring than that. But the money did make this class more than just an exercise; many students were serious about starting a business.

The discussions around their businesses and the crisis in the industry led us to perform research about new business models for news, modeling what the business of a metropolitan ecosystem of news would look like after the death of the daily paper (not that we'd wish for such an occurrence, but so we could examine what the ecosystem — from beat businesses to new news organizations to networks — could provide). This work was done by Jennifer McFadden, Nancy Wang, and Jeff Mignon, led by Tow-Knight's Peter Hauck. We presented the work at a Knight Foundation event at the Aspen Institute in 2009.[126]

In Aspen, Alberto Ibargüen, president and CEO of the Knight Foundation, asked our founding dean, Steve Shepard, what his new school would stand for uniquely. Steve replied: entrepreneurial journalism. Knight soon matched a generous, $3-million challenge grant from Leonard Tow and Emily Tow Jackson at the Tow Foundation, allowing us to create the Tow-Knight Center for Entrepreneurial Journalism. We then had the great fortune to bring in Jeremy Caplan, a journalist and a holder of an MBA from Columbia, to spearhead the educational work of the entrepreneurial program, creating the nation's first M.A. and an Advanced Certificate in Entrepreneurial Journalism.

Jeremy is a wonderful and hard-working teacher who keeps cramming more learning into the program. He teaches a course that offers in essence an MBA-in-a-box in the context of media. He arranges meetings and discussions at an amazing list of New York start-ups in media and technology. He recruits mentors for every student and we both take great advantage of working in the center of the universe, bringing in an enviable list of guest speakers from New York's media and technology communities to share their experience and advice. Jeremy also recruits experts to teach workshops in technology skills. If students need special skills, they may take classes at General Assembly, a coworking space turned school for entrepreneurs. Together, Jeremy and I meet with the students as a group to discuss issues, such as the ethics of being both church and state in a startup, and to collaboratively solve students' problems. My favorite part of teaching at CUNY is the time I get to spend one-on-one with these students at the whiteboard, identifying their opportunities and problems and next tasks. I think of it as being on a dozen startup boards. Jeremy handles the recruiting. We have found that the best students come into the program with an idea for a business. But the best students also often change that idea when confronted with the real needs of real customers or the reality of competition or a new opportunity that presents itself. In entrepreneurship, as in journalism itself, the key skill we must teach today is the ability to listen and to change. As I write this, we are also planning to offer specialized and intensive three-week training in how to start and run a beat business.

I am pleased to report that eight years after starting our first class in entrepreneurial journalism, we held an event at CUNY for others teaching in the field in 2014 and had about 60 professors in attendance and more watching online. The field we helped start is growing.

Tow-Knight also has a mission to conduct useful research, benefitting both the industry and our students. Dr. Nick Diakopoulos examined the unexplored opportunities for new technologies in news and created a brainstorming game for use by students at CUNY and elsewhere and also for media executives.[127] Peter Hauck ran a study looking at the digital presences of 1,000 local merchants and services in a neighborhood of New York and a town in New Jersey, revealing many opportunities for local media companies to help customers improve their online efforts.[128] Now Tow-Knight's Hal Straus is managing the creation of a series of papers on best practices for local beat businesses — in advertising products and services, sales techniques, marketing, events, and print.[129] And I have been devoting a great deal of my time to working in the local news ecosystems of New Jersey as well as New York to try to find ways to sustain, improve, and grow them. I described much of that work and its lessons thus far earlier in this essay. In New Jersey, I have been working with the Dodge Foundation — Chris Daggett, Molly de Aguiar, and Josh Stearns — and Montclair State University — Debbie Galant, Ju-Don Marshall Roberts, and Merrill Brown — and in New York with CUNY's Center for Community and Ethnic Media, run by my colleague, Garry Pierre-Pierre.

Now to forms: I would say that we — at CUNY and in journalism schools across the country — have been remiss in not doing more to invent and incubate development of new forms of news. If anyone should support innovation and if anyone can afford to experiment and fail, it is universities. But we face a paradox in professional schools at a time of disruption in our field: Students still come to schools such as ours to learn the fundamentals and the eternal verities of the craft, as our founding dean, Steve Shepard, puts it.

They aspire to be what they see rather than what they cannot yet imagine. They still get jobs in the field as it is. And so we must prepare them for that. But we also must prepare them as leaders, as inventors and entrepreneurs, and as disruptors themselves. We have found at CUNY that a three-semester program (plus a paid, summer internship) is barely enough time to teach all that we must teach. How do we carve out time to challenge the thinking behind some of the skills we have just taught so they can invent surprising new ways to accomplish journalism's mission?

We do have opportunities for innovation in our curriculum: My colleague Sandeep Junnarkar and the teachers he leads in our interactive program encourage students to bring all relevant media tools to bear to tell their stories in new ways. My colleague Steve Strasser is moving the student magazine he runs, 219 Magazine, to Medium so students can work in a new form, find an audience, and be motivated to think graphically. And Travis Fox, the head of our visual journalism program, is instituting a course in reinventing TV news with professors Bob Sacha and Simon Surowicz at the same time that Tow-Knight is starting a series of events to offer visions for what TV news could be.

Finally, to relationships: Since our school began and I started in our interactive program with Sandeep Junnarkar, I have said that we had one fundamental challenge: It is difficult to teach students interactive journalism when they don't have a community with whom to interact. In the old days, when I attended journalism school, we wrote our stories for an audience of one: the professor. Now, students can indeed reach the public online. But one can't just gin up a community out of nowhere. This is why Eric Newton of the Knight Foundation champions the teaching hospital model for journalism schools — not only so students get experience working on real stories but more importantly so they can serve and be answerable to real communities. We tried to address this at CUNY when we started The Local, a blog serving Fort Greene, Brooklyn, in partnership with The New York Times. That proved to be both too small and too challenging for many reasons. We have been looking at more ways to open various teaching hospital wards.

Then, on a trip to California to introduce our new dean, Sarah Bartlett, to technology leaders including Reid Hoffman, founder of LinkedIn and a partner at the venture capital firm Greylock Capital; Dick Costolo, CEO of Twitter; Ev Williams, cofounder of Blogger, Twitter, and now Medium; the strategy team at Google; Craig Newmark; and others, I subjected her to a draft of the first part of this essay, on relationships. She got off the plane and said she didn't disagree with my thesis about reimagining journalism as a service business built on relationships. But then she asked whether I thought we were teaching that in depth at CUNY. She suggested creating a new degree.

In January 2015, pending New York State approval, we will offer the first M.A. in Social Journalism, the study and practice of engaged communities in the time of social media, under the direction of Dr. Carrie Brown, formerly of the University of Memphis.[130] You have just read the thinking behind that program. It will include two courses in listening (starting with the community and its needs rather than our content), two in journalism (reporting collaboratively), two in data (data as a means of listening, data as news, data as a means of judging impact and success), and two in tools (how to understand the dynamics of how people use such platforms as Twitter), with an intense business training, and a full-time, mentored practicum working in the community each student elects to serve (whether that community is based on geography, demographics, interests, needs, or even an event — real or virtual). We will also conduct research and hold events in engagement and journalism.

I've described only the ways in which the thinking in this essay is borne out in our programs at CUNY. Obviously, these are just slices of our program, which changes constantly around new needs and opportunities. We face the challenges every journalism school faces today: how to teach change; how to teach enough tools so students leave proficient in them without letting that rob vital time from the teaching of the basic skills and verities of journalism; how to stay ahead of change in the field while still preparing students for the jobs that exist today. It's not easy. But there is no better time to teach journalism and no better time to become a journalist. Youth, I tell my students, used to be something to get over. Now youth is an asset. Our students today are not only more technically skilled than we could be, they see the world in new ways. I urge them to guard that fresh perspective and to use it to question and challenge all of our assumptions so they can imagine and build a new future for journalism.

ACKNOWLEDGMENTS AND DISCLOSURES

I would like to thank my deans — the journalism school's founding dean and my dear friend, Steve Shepard; our new dean and my great partner, Sarah Bartlett; and our associate dean and my wise and patient guide, Judy Watson — for encouraging me to start and goading me to finish this essay. I am grateful to my Tow-Knight colleagues — Jeremy Caplan, Carrie Brown, Peter Hauck, Hal Straus, Chris Anderson, Lori Robinson, Dawn Barber — and our many collaborators, among them Jennifer McFadden, Nancy Wang, Jeff Mignon, Paul Noglows, Nick Diakopoulos, Annaliese Griffin, and too many to list. I am also grateful to my interactive colleague, Sandeep Junnarkar, and all my faculty colleagues, who both tolerate and contribute to my crazy notions.

I can't give enough thanks to Leonard Tow and Emily Tow Jackson as well as Andrea Sholler of the Tow Foundation, for betting on our new school and challenging us to build the center that bears the Tow name. I am indebted to the Knight Foundation — Alberto Ibargüen, Michael Maness, Eric Newton, Marie Gilot, John Bracken, and Bahia Ramos — for supporting not only Tow-Knight but also the first major research that led to the center's creation. I am also grateful to them for supporting the Knight Innovation Awards at CUNY, our new degree in Social Journalism, and the work I do with the Dodge Foundation in New Jersey. In New Jersey, I want to thank the head of

Dodge, my friend and neighbor, Chris Daggett, and Dodge's media visionary, Molly de Aguiar, and Josh Stearns. I am honored that Reid Hoffman saw fit to support the development of our Social Journalism M.A. and to help us think about the future of our field. And I want to thank the McCormick, MacArthur, and Scripps foundations and the Carnegie Corporation of New York as well as John Paton and John Thornton for further support.

Finally, I owe much to the companies I work with for grounding me in the reality of their challenges and opportunities: John Paton and Jim Brady at Digital First Media; Matt Kraner, Lamar Graham, Randy Siegel, Steve Newhouse, and Michael Newhouse at Advance; Alan Rusbridger, Andrew Miller, and so many others at the Guardian; as well as members of CUNY's Journalism School advisory board. I thank my journalism-school comrades from outside CUNY — Jay Rosen, Clay Shirky, Emily Bell, Dan Gillmor, Owen Youngman, Merrill Brown, and others from too many conferences and too many hours on Twitter — for their inspiration and education. I thank my CUNY colleague Tim Harper and our CUNY Journalism Press partner John Oakes as well as his colleagues Courtney Andujar, Emily Freyer, and Matthew Schantz for their help in publishing this tome. And thank you, Les Hinton, for inspiring the title.

As a matter of disclosure, I have recently advised Digital First Media, Advance Publications, and the Guardian and in the past I have advised or spoken at events held by the Telegraph, Burda, Axel Springer, Stern, About.com for The New York Times Company, Holtzbrinck, Hearst, Meredith, The Week, Sky News, and others. Also in the past, I have worked full-time for Advance.net, the online arm of Advance Publications; News Corp. at TV Guide and Delphi Internet Services; the New York Daily News; Entertainment Weekly and People Weekly at Time Inc.; the San Francisco Examiner at Hearst; and the Chicago Tribune and Chicago Today at Tribune

Company. I own or have recently owned stocks including Time Warner and its many spinoffs, Google, Amazon, and Microsoft. Also please see buzzmachine.com/about for further disclosures of professional relationships.

NOTES

1. http://www.scribd.com/doc/23476823/Speech-from-Les-Hinton-Dow-Jones-CEO-to-World-Association-of-Newspapers-conference
2. *The Story So Far: What We Know About the Business of Digital Journalism* by Bill Grueskin, Ava Seave, and Lucas Graves, Columbia Journalism Review, May 10, 2011: http://www.cjr.org/the_business_of_digital_journalism/introduction. php See also *The Reconstruction of American Journalism* by Michael Schudson and Leonard Downie, Columbia Journalism Review, October 19, 2009: http://www.cjr.org/reconstruction/the_reconstruction_of_american.php
3. Post-Industrial Journalism: Adapting to the Present by Chris Anderson, Emily Bell, and Clay Shirky: http://towcenter.org/research/post-industrial-journalism/
4. http://www.poynter.org/latest-news/top-stories/198970/how-the-new-york-times-snow-fall-project-unifies-text-multimedia/
5. http://www.thewire.com/technology/2012/12/new-york-times-snow-fall-feature/60219/
6. http://www.nytimes.com/projects/2012/snow-fall/#/?part=tunnel-creek
7. Confidence Game by Dean Starkman, Columbia Journalism Review, November/December 2011 http://www.cjr.org/essay/confidence_game.php?page=all
8. A report on the Baruch event here: http://www.capitalnewyork.com/article/media/2012/05/5827045/its-year-1472-journalism-fact-some-people-and-some-dont
9. Jay Rosen's blog post coining the phrase: http://archive.pressthink.org/2006/06/27/ppl_frmr.html
10. http://memex.naughtons.org/wp-content/uploads/2013/01/A-Brief-History-of-the-Future-Chapter10.html
11. Thanks to Jay Rosen for teaching me this. Higgins, John H., ed. *The Raymond Williams Reader*. Malden, Mass.: Blackwell, 2001. p 46
12. http://www.hindustantimes.com/india-news/tina-brown-doesn-t-read-magazines-anymore/article1-1148890.aspx
13. "We will learn we are part of something new, that our readers/listeners/viewers are becoming part of the process. I take it for granted, for example, that my readers know more than I do—and this is a liberating, not threatening, fact of journalistic life. Every reporter on every beat should embrace this." — Dan Gillmor, *We the Media*, O'Reilly, 2004. http://www.authorama.com/we-the-media-1.html Gillmor has often corrected those who misquote him as saying that the public is smarter then he is.
14. From *What Would Google Do?*: http://buzzmachine.com/2012/02/01/facebook-goes-public-zuckerberg-in-public-parts-wwgd/
15. https://plus.google.com/u/1/102034052532213921839/posts/NJzHsuVQvAu
16. http://www.poynter.org/latest-news/top-stories/225139/pew-surveys-of-audience-habits-suggest-perilous-future-for-news/
17. http://www.niemanlab.org/2013/07/gawker-is-letting-readers-rewrite-head-lines-and-reframe-articles/
18. http://archive.pressthink.org/2004/01/07/press_religion.html
19. http://www.mediabistro.com/fishbowldc/confirmed-len-downie-registers-to-vote_b13214

20. Storyify of that Twitter discussion: https://storify.com/antderosa/reinventing-the-article
21. http://buzzmachine.com/2012/05/26/news-articles-assets-paths/
22. http://scripting.com/river/?panel=dave
23. http://twitpic.com/135xa
24. http://www.vocativ.com/about/
25. http://blog.safecast.org/about/
26. http://www.kickstarter.com/projects/seanbonner/safecast-x-kickstarter-geiger-counter?ref=live
27. http://www.cnbc.com/id/101469500
28. http://www.huffingtonpost.com/arianna-huffington/journalism-2009-desperate_b_374642.html
29. http://online.wsj.com/news/articles/SB10001424052748704107104574569570797550520
30. http://blogs.wsj.com/economics/2012/07/05/is-data-is-or-is-data-aint-a-plural/
31. http://piktochart.com/gallery/themes/#all
32. http://www.poynter.org/latest-news/top-stories/121281/texas-tribune-databases-drive-majority-of-sites-traffic-help-citizens-make-sense-of-government-data/
33. See Lawrence Lessig's essay on the risks of transparency as a weapon: http://www.newrepublic.com/article/books-and-arts/against-transparency
34. Google Trends search: http://www.google.com/trends/
35. http://www.vox.com/2014/7/18/5915193/a-greater-share-of-netherlands-population-was-killed-than-the-us
36. In the U.K., phone company O2 released stats showing how people use their smartphones: 25:49 minutes per day on the internet, 17:29 on social media, 15:38 on music, 14:26 on games, and only 12:06 on phone calls (plus additional time on emails, texting, TV/film, books, and taking pictures). http://www.telegraph.co.uk/technology/mobile-phones/9365085/Smartphones-hardly-used-for-calls.html
37. For a much longer discussion of issues around privacy and personal data, see my book, "Public Parts: How Sharing in the Digital Age Improves the Way We Live and Work."
38. http://www.subtraction.com/2014/04/18/are-magazine-apps-dead/
39. http://bits.blogs.nytimes.com/2014/04/16/can-facebook-innovate-a-conversation-with-mark-zuckerberg/
40. http://arstechnica.com/science/2014/02/science-confirms-online-trolls-are-horrible-people-also-sadists/
41. http://www.hollywoodreporter.com/live-feed/cnns-jeff-zucker-interview-show-695133
42. http://thenextweb.com/google/2012/04/08/virtual-photo-walks-on-google-allow-the-sick-and-disabled-to-explore-the-world/
43. http://mashable.com/2014/05/09/cnn-obsessed-malaysia-mh370-zucker/
44. http://www.towknight.org/research/newopps/
45. Information for playing the game available here: http://www.towknight.org/aha/
46. Here is Google Executive Chairman Eric Schmidt with a variation on that theme: http://www.politico.com/news/stories/0410/35649.html
47. http://www.gallup.com/poll/171740/americans-confidence-news-media-remains-low.aspx
48. Disclosure: I have been a member of Paton's advisory board; additional disclosures appear at the end of this essay.
49. http://buzzmachine.com/2011/11/03/digital-first/
50. http://buzzmachine.com/2006/03/27/your-homework/
51. http://adage.com/article/digital/emarketer-facebook-microsoft-pass-yahoo-s-u-s-ad-share/245761/
52. http://www.niemanlab.org/riptide/chapter-4-the-original-sin/

53. http://www.aei-ideas.org/2014/04/creative-destruction-2013-newspaper-ad-revenue-continued-its-precipitous-free-fall-and-its-probably-not-over-yet/
54. http://newsosaur.blogspot.com/2013/11/are-newspapers-losing-mass-media-mojo.html Alan Mutter estimates even lower penetration numbers here: http://newsosaur.blogspot.com/2014/07/the-newspaper-crisis-by-numbers.html
55. According to Pew, legal notices together with obituaries — "other" in the chart at this link — now account for more revenue than any of the three old classified-ad categories: auto, real estate, jobs. http://stateofthemedia.org/2013/newspapers-stabilizing-but-still-threatened/5-real-estate-classified-ads-dip-most-in-2012/
56. http://stateofthemedia.org/2013/news-magazines-embracing-their-digital-future/news-magazines-by-the-numbers/
57. http://stateofthemedia.org/2013/local-tv-audience-declines-as-revenue-bounces-back/local-tv-by-the-numbers/
58. http://online.wsj.com/articles/gm-p-g-cutting-back-their-tv-ad-commitments-1405699483
59. http://mashable.com/2014/05/16/full-new-york-times-innovation-report/
60. http://query.nytimes.com/mem/archive-free/pdf?res=9B02E7D6143FE433A25750C0A9679D946097D6CF
61. Here is a related, brief essay on my technological transition in the news business: https://medium.com/change-objects/goodbye-ctrl-s-8f424e463dbe
62. The line began with a slight variation: http://buzzmachine.com/2007/02/22/new-rule-cover-what-you-do-best-link-to-the-rest/
63. http://globalvoicesonline.org/
64. The job title disappeared before gender sensitivity could have had the opportunity to mangle it into rewritepersons.
65. http://asne.org/blog_home.asp?Display=1729
66. http://www.towknight.org/research/models/
67. For a comprehensive list of local sites with much data about them see Michele's List, which is now supported by the Tow-Knight Center: http://www.micheleslist.org/
68. It will be found at http://towknight.org/research
69. http://www.towknight.org/research/beyondbanners/
70. http://www.niemanlab.org/2013/09/what-makes-the-texas-tribunes-event-business-so-successful/
71. In a 2006 meeting of journalists from organizations large and small held in Philadelphia before its newspapers were sold into a hell of mogul bondage, this entity, the new news organization, was christened the "norg" by Will Bunch, an organizer of the event and a columnist and blogger for the city's Daily News. I will give him credit and blame for the term as is due. http://buzzmachine.com/2006/03/25/saving-journalism-and-killing-the-press/
72. http://www.towknight.org/research/models/
73. According to Millward Brown: http://www.brandz100.com/site/home.php?t=article&id=148
74. http://marketingland.com/get-programmatic-primer-programmatic-advertising-94502
75. https://www.adroll.com/retargeting
76. http://buzzmachine.com/2013/05/15/selling-ads-by-time-not-space/
77. http://www.thedrum.com/news/2014/05/22/financial-times-kicks-trials-sell-advertisers-blocks-time-tackle-industry-s
78. Public Parts: How Sharing in the Digital Age Improves the Way We Work and Live. http://buzzmachine.com/publicparts/
79. http://online.wsj.com/public/page/what-they-know-digital-privacy.html
80. http://paidpost.nytimes.com/netflix/women-inmates-separate-but-not-equal.html
81. http://time.com/12933/what-you-think-you-know-about-the-web-is-wrong/

82. http://www.iab.net/media/file/IAB_Edelman_Berland_Study.pdf
83. https://www.quantcast.com/buzzfeed.com
84. http://www.usatoday.com/story/money/columnist/wolff/2014/08/17/buzzfeed-huffington-post/14076989/
85. http://www.bloomberg.com/news/2014-08-12/buzzfeed-s-valuation-tops-tribune-s-validates-approach.html
86. http://www.buzzfeed.com/mlew15/19-cats-who-are-definitely-planning-to-murder-you-h0se
87. See also Steve Waldman's discussion about the limits of the listicle model as journalism's salvation: http://www.washingtonmonthly.com/magazine/junejulyaugust_2014/ten_miles_square/can_listicles_fund_the_baghdad050663.php
88. http://www.forbes.com/sites/kashmirhill/2012/02/16/how-target-figured-out-a-teen-girl-was-pregnant-before-her-father-did/
89. http://www.theatlantic.com/technology/archive/2014/08/advertising-is-the-internets-original-sin/376041/?single_page=true
90. http://www.cjr.org/essay/confidence_game.php?page=all
91. http://audio.wbur.org/storage/2011/03/onpoint_0328_paywall-debate.mp3
92. http://www.niemanlab.org/riptide/chapter-4-the-original-sin/
93. http://investors.nytco.com/investors/investor-news/investor-news-details/2014/The-New-York-Times-Company-Reports-2014-Second-Quarter-Results/default.aspx
94. See Nisenholtz' interview on original sin and much more as part of the Riptide project he helped organize: http://www.niemanlab.org/riptide/person/martin-nisenholtz/
95. http://investors.nytco.com/press/press-releases/press-release-details/2013/The-New-York-Times-Announces-Solid-Circulation-Gains-/default.aspx
96. http://www.niemanlab.org/2014/05/if-my-newspaper-puts-up-a-metered-paywall-how-many-people-will-pay-heres-some-data/
97. http://www.editorandpublisher.com/Features/Article/A-Look-At-How-Gannett-s-Digital-Strategies-Are-Paying-Off
98. http://www.poynter.org/latest-news/top-stories/237601/gannett-earnings-report-hints-at-a-coming-problem-with-paywalls/
99. http://investors.nytco.com/files/doc_news/2014/Press-Release-6-29-2014-FI-NAL-330-Monday.pdf
100. I speculated about this on my blog in December 2011; you can read the discussion there: http://buzzmachine.com/2011/12/19/why-not-a-reverse-meter/ At almost the same time, News Corp.'s Raju Narisetti proposed a "why don't we pay you paywall": http://www.slideshare.net/mathewi/raju-narisettis-freewall-presentation-at-newsfoo
101. https://www.kickstarter.com/discover/categories/journalism
102. http://www.theguardian.com/membership/2014/sep/10/-sp-guardian-editor-alan-rusbridger-welcome-to-guardian-membership
103. http://informerly.com/
104. https://twitter.com/vivian/timelines/505375883063230465
105. http://en.wikipedia.org/wiki/Paradox_of_value
106. Here is Dr. Peter Higgs explaining the Higgs Boson on the BBC. Now because the BBC asked the question and presented the answer on its air, it owns the copyright — though, of course, the knowledge comes directly from Dr. Higgs. https://www.youtube.com/watch?v=Nrf3wO1pR1s
107. http://sb.longnow.org/SB_homepage/Info_free_story.html
108. http://www.story-tour.com/
109. http://narrative.ly/
110. http://www.tinabrownmedia.com/about-us/
111. Though this book is available for free online because my and my school's goal is to promote discussion of the ideas in it.

112. There are new syndication platforms such as Newscred (which bought a startup where I was a partner, Daylife) and there are content creation and sales companies such as Contently and Narrative.ly. So it might seem that content syndication is alive and well. Note that some of Newscred's customers are sites that aggregate content, such as Business Insider; by paying for content from a news organization it tends to keep the legal dogs at bay when Business Insider also curates and summarizes that news organization's work. Newscred's other customer base — like those of both Contently and Narrative.ly — are nonmedia brands that now think they must enter media; they want content of their own to wrap their messages around or to carry their messages.
113. http://repubhub.icopyright.net/
114. http://time.com/12933/what-you-think-you-know-about-the-web-is-wrong/
115. Munson and Warren, James Carey: A Critical Reader
116. Eisenstein, Elizabeth, *The Printing Press as an Agent of Change*, p. 33
117. Pettegree, Andrew, *The Invention of News: How The World Came to Know About Itself*, p. 168
118. Pettegree, p. 8-9
119. Osterhammel, Jürgen, *The Transformation of the World: A Global History of the Nineteenth Century*, p. 138
120. ibid., p. 312
121. http://amzn.to/1nO9QTA
122. http://www.bloomberg.com/news/2013-03-08/news-corp-publishing-starts-with-2-6-billion-cash.html
123. http://buzzmachine.com/2005/12/05/the-last-presses/
124. See a discussion on the topic here: http://buzzmachine.com/2014/08/14/dystopia-com/
125. http://www.fcc.gov/info-needs-communities
126. http://www.towknight.org/models/
127. http://www.towknight.org/research/newopps/
128. http://www.towknight.org/research/beyondbanners/
129. These will be made available at http://www.towknight.org/research/
130. https://medium.com/whither-news/social-journalism-39c0edce8a9

CUNY JOURNALISM PRESS

The CUNY Journalism Press is the academic publishing imprint of the CUNY Graduate School of Journalism. Part of the City University of New York, the CUNY Journalism Press publishes both traditional print books and e-books about journalists and journalism. We welcome inquiries about our books and our authors, and we welcome proposals for future books from prospective authors. See more at: www.press.journalism.cuny.edu

The Press was launched in the autumn of 2012 with the mission of publishing serious books about journalism and the news media — history, theory, criticism, craft, memoir and more. The Press is organized, in conjunction with the independent publishing house OR Books, as a new model for publishing — some call it co-publishing — in response to changes in the publishing marketplace and publishing technology. Our aim is to publish books by, for and about journalists that might not otherwise be published in the commercial marketplace.

The CUNY Graduate School of Journalism, widely known for its emphasis on multimedia, interactive and cross-platform reporting and storytelling, offers an intensive three-semester Master of Arts in Journalism curriculum. The school is also known for its innovative training in emerging technology and its Tow-Knight Center for Entrepreneurial Journalism, dedicated to finding new business models. The school is the first in the world to offer an M.A. in Entrepreneurial Journalism, and is planning to add an M.A. in Social Journalism beginning in 2015. See more at www.journalism.cuny.edu

ALSO PUBLISHED BY CUNY JOURNALISM PRESS

DISTANT WITNESS
SOCIAL MEDIA, THE ARAB SPRING AND A JOURNALISM REVOLUTION
by Andy Carvin
ISBN 978-1-939293-02-2 (paperback)
ISBN 978-1-939293-03-9 (e-book)

FIGHTING FOR THE PRESS
THE INSIDE STORY OF THE PENTAGON PAPERS AND OTHER BATTLES
by James Goodale
ISBN 978-1-939293-12-1 (hardcover)
ISBN 978-1-939293-08-4 (paperback)
ISBN 978-1-939293-09-1 (e-book)

CITIZENS RISING
INDEPENDENT JOURNALISM AND THE SPREAD OF DEMOCRACY
by David Hoffman
ISBN 978-1-939293-29-9 (paperback)
ISBN 978-1-939293-30-5 (e-book)

THE PLEASURES OF BEING OUT OF STEP
NAT HENTOFF'S LIFE IN JOURNALISM, JAZZ AND THE FIRST AMENDMENT
by David L. Lewis
ISBN 978-1-939293-19-0 (paperback)
ISBN 978-1-939293-20-6 (e-book)

THE ILLUSTRATED COURTROOM: 50 YEARS OF COURT ART
by Elizabeth Williams and Sue Russell
ISBN 978-1-939293-52-7 (paperback)
ISBN 978-1-939293-53-4 (e-book)

JEFF JARVIS is a professor at the City University of New York Graduate School of Journalism, where he directs the Tow-Knight Center for Entrepreneurial Journalism. He is the author of two prior books — *What Would Google Do?* and *Public Parts: How Sharing in the Digital Age Improves the Way We Work and Live* — in addition to the e-book *Gutenberg the Geek*. He blogs at Buzzmachine.com and is a cohost of the podcast "This Week in Google."

Jarvis, one of the preeminent voices on emerging forms of journalism, news delivery, and community engagement, advises many media companies, startups, and foundations. From 2007 to 2014, he has been named one of the world's 100 media leaders by the World Economic Forum at Davos. He was also creator and founding editor of Entertainment Weekly; president and creative director of Advance.net, the online arm of Advance Publications; Sunday editor and associate publisher of the New York Daily News; TV critic for TV Guide and People; a columnist on The San Francisco Examiner; and a reporter and editor on the Chicago Tribune.